W9-AWZ-383

NEUROTICS
in the
Church

ROBERT JAMES ST. CLAIR

FLEMING H. REVELL COMPANY

To my wife, RUTH
and to
my two boys, PAUL and JAMES

FOREWORD

"The primary drives are hunger, sex and thirst," said the old text, and it has taken us a while to discover that people can do with a minimum of all three because their real drive is to gain status with God or the world. We have taken "status" to be a rather dirty word. It reminds us of the competitive bragging of poor nomads on the Sahara Desert. Actually, civilization wouldn't have much stability without status. The father at the table, the big chief at the lodge meeting, the witch doctor in the tribe, all have position. Everyone feels safer if he knows his position in the scheme of things, and he can respect other positions without too much anxiety about his own. We look down on the Indian caste system, but in America or Britain a man may work most of his life to gain exalted status only to find his enjoyment of it delayed by nervous breakdowns and heart attacks. In India a man is born into his position; there is no need for him to drive himself to drink changing it, and that is that.

Here in America the structure of society is supposed to be quite simple. The prestige of race, place of birth, beauty, brains, talent —each has value in some circles, but the dollar bill is a coupon redeemable anywhere for almost anything. A price tag is an easy measuring stick of prestige. The female wearer of mink is several notches higher than one wearing lamb's wool—and not only higher, but safer and stronger and happier. Well, maybe not, but in a free capitalistic society a man with an education, good health, shrewdness, connections and the ability to work seventy hours a week can change both his bank account and his status. If he doesn't have the first four qualifications, it doesn't make that much difference. And if he lacks all five he can still be born to a father who had them and who passed on his status through his last will and testament. The whole idea may be fallacious but it isn't about to be abolished by each generation that has a chance to try it out.

We seem to be at a point now where the adventure in status-climbing in everything from southern buses to Protestant churches is being studied. When Harry Golden, Vance Packard and Gibson Winter say the whole scheme is laid on the altar to be sanctified, they aren't far wrong.

"It was within this same quarter of a century that the South lost its Bible Belt coloration and today the laymen have taken over— the trustees, the elders, the fellows in the economic power structure of the city." This fact holds more than a grain of truth. When the Apostles ordained elders and deacons they never dreamed of the fiasco these status-orders would create—and not only today, but right after the Reformation when the rising middle class demanded power commensurate with their money and quietly announced to their bishops some version of "No taxation without representation!" It is automatically assumed that the new vice-president of the large corporation will be elected to the official board holding the reigns of power, and few in the congregation would object on the grounds of spiritual deficiency.

The junior executives of the same firm are the first to assume that their executive will wear the post like a glove. And the executive assumes that the junior fellows are Big Givers and are coming up through the ranks via the board of deacons, the trustees and finally the elders. In smaller churches where the frustrated layman enjoys top billing on the chief board, he is not about to entertain competition from ambitious newcomers. Consequently the lesser board, such as the deacons, is either non-existent or safely reserved for the "very religious" who wish to serve without ruling.

We all love to watch *others* run the ragged race, and especially now when a quiet revolution is mixing up the symbols. It's getting so you can hardly tell who's on first without a program. The symbols used to be fins on the car, then bigger fins, then midget foreign cars, then three cars, then one Cadillac and one strange foreign job. In some places the new status symbol is no TV. Then there are gold golf tees and motorized toothbrushes for those who have status-without-status by disdaining status.

The man at the bottom of the ladder may feel hopeless—but there is always the church. It even announces salvation without trying for it! He may only get on the board of trustees of the Baptist Church, but with the right requirements of spirit he may make the top board of the Pentecostal Church. In fact he can reject the worldly values of his neighbors and become the right hand of the Mind that rules the world. The lodge and the club are man-made, but the church is divine. Some day the saints will rule the world. After all, how much status can you take?

Much of our spiritual dilemma is the product of the institutional caste system, but oversimplification only tries to force a two-cylinder fact to pull an eight-cylinder conviction. No doubt the jockeying for position, the persecution of the poor fellow who disrupted the peace, and the election of officers each have a part in the bickering going on in every free and independent church. But there has been a lingering suspicion in my own mind that in many cases the trouble goes far deeper. Trouble can fall on a congregation and shake its life until it lies limp.

We cannot lay all the trouble at the doors of religious potentates. One pastor wept for a few nights when a meek hotel doorman, who had only his gold braids to keep his status warm, was elected to the board of stewards. Suddenly the doorman became a roaring tyrant glaring down at the pastor. But with grace and patience that problem was handled by the Holy Spirit and the doorman became a dynamo.

Nor is the disaster of crippled congregations always caused by the lay urgency to reproduce the social strata in church by barring Negroes, members of the blue-collar class, and aspiring sheep from the sects. Nor is the trouble usually caused by ministers who associate with Negroes only to find some startled laymen have requested a denominational committee to rattle his security.

Any study of the religious neurotic as an isolated entity is totally inadequate. According to Dr. Karen Horney, neurotic disturbances must be viewed against the background of the human being's cultural setting and social values. Since society's values have come to be such determining factors in both church and government, any approach to therapy of the religious neurotic must always be made within the wider framework of church-culture relationship. If we are to cope with the disturbed person, we must try to understand some of the mixture of spiritual and neurotic motivations entering into his behavior.

Getting the attention of the churches on the roots of trouble is almost as difficult as finding the roots in the first place. Let a note be pinned on the grapevine that Reverend So-and-so is having trouble in his church. Ministers will shake their heads in sober self-righteousness and laymen will huddle in a corner to garner the salient and perchance gory details. No wonder, despite courageous sermons on how much God loves us, so many pastors decide that if the status quo cannot be shaken, then it's better to shore it up and guard the peace at any price.

At first it seems impossible to trace any roots at all. It is not too easy to find cases to study. At the first slight tremor in the foundation many a minister pushes the panic button and interprets the alarm as a call by the Holy Spirit to move along. And in case he doesn't hear anything there is always some nervous and slightly unscrupulous denominational representative who will barge in and push the button for him.

When the tremor grows to an earthquake, leaving a cleavage down the center of the congregation, we can find a pattern that is duplicated, with slight variations, from New York to Los Angeles.

A mythical *Handbook of All Problems in Church,* covering every cause of disturbance, could never be written. The task here is to study the personality factors and the psychological dynamics of these cleavages against the social background of which we have been speaking. We must find a system that will bridge the gap between neurotic personalities, who provide the explosive power to keep these tremors active, and the social and theological weaknesses in churches, which allow them to grow to devastating dimensions.

Such a system must take into account our social values. It is not hard to understand why. The neurotic personality has taken our prestige system and galvanized it into a formidable security complex. In him the drives for gaining status have gone to seed, and he defends a glorified image of himself for which he seeks authentication in church. He uses religious ideas to defend his position at all costs. He resists social and religious change. He is wary of threats from competitors, from the pastor, and from the very prophetic nature of the church that seeks to measure all by the love and holiness of God.

The so-called *normal* individual knows the values of his culture and has a realistic view of his abilities and loveworthiness. The *immature* person lacks adeptness in meeting society's demands and is not yet sure of his acceptance and value to others. The *neurotic* person is deeply disturbed in his relations with others. He makes a contract with society whereby he is such an all-wise, all-knowing, absolutely perfect (or thoroughly loving) person that he *deserves* full obedience, honor and acceptance.

We can take the psychological norm from the person of Christ. As Son of man, He is the example of true humanity. As Son of God, He mediates the saving personality of the objective God who, when embraced in experience, enables the new man to be uniquely and thoroughly his individual self. Unfortunately the gray area between normal and neurotic persons is wide indeed.

When the influence of neurotic persons spreads, it means the very air crackles with the sensitivities of guarded rights and privileges. Beneath the layer of gaiety and charm there is, in a neurotic church, a hotbed of vindictiveness ready to explode when someone steps out of line. Instead of being therapeutic to the world, the neurotic church aggravates symptoms and draws more neurotic persons into it.

At the present time sincere believers are praying and studying to rediscover the power and mission of the church. Great obstacles are in the way, and some understanding of neurosis in the church is one of many major steps that must be taken on the road that leads forward. A clearer understanding of disguised idolatry in ourselves, in our churches and in the world will free the people of Christ to be ministered unto and to minister in His name.

ACKNOWLEDGMENT

I would like to thank all the ministers and laymen who granted interviews. With a few exceptions I have changed some details to mask identities.

For the past several years Dr. Roy Burkhart worked to help disturbed churches and pastors. In assisting me he could be a severe critic and a gentle shepherd. I eagerly awaited his word on my completed manuscript, but on December 9, 1962, he was taken to heaven. His constant prodding, "What about remedies? What about remedies?" makes me believe his satisfaction will depend on whether persons and churches invest themselves in a richer experience of life.

Betty Biesterveld, whose book *Run, Reddy, Run* was recently published, is a dear friend and member of our church. Her prodding and encouragement helped in midstream when I was equally distant from each bank and the waters were deepest.

I owe the most to my wife Ruth. She has a keen grasp of the problems and the psychology of the abnormal personality. The same uncompromising honesty she brings to all of life was brought to my manuscript. A man is fortunate when he has a friend who believes strongly in God and believes deeply in him.

CONTENTS

CONTENTS

1
Sick Churches and a Lost Mission

WHEN SO MANY CHRISTIANS THROUGHOUT THE WORLD FOCUS their attention on the same problem at the same time, the need for action must be urgent and obvious. The church, the people of God in Christ's mission, finds her mission hazy and her numbers immobilized.

In theory, at least, the church as a whole knows what she is about. There is no lack of study guides, based solidly on Scripture, defining the task of lay and clerical apostles. The church is to be the Body of the continuing ministry of Jesus. Through this Body He reconciles men to God that the Holy Spirit may do His eternal work in their hearts and sanctify their hands to His labors.

The church is Christ's sanctuary to raise a united voice of praise and song to His glory. Through her ministry, forgiven sinners receive the revelation of God. By her hands, healing, clothing and feeding express compassion in His holy name. Hers is the prophetic voice of His eternal Spirit crashing against all that hinders the enlargement of His Kingdom. Judgment is spoken and men are called to repent and flee to Christ, for the world's night is coming when no man can work and the holy sovereignty of God is vindicated and every tongue must confess that Christ is Lord to the glory of the Father. In the midst of the world's pride and lavish splendor the church has a seemingly incredible pronouncement: the kingdoms of this world are become the Kingdoms of our Lord and of His Christ.

The church is comfortable today. In a self-conscious, self-indulgent and too-comfortable world the church is not too inclined to stop and ask herself what she is singing. If Christ is pictured as a cheerful, middle-class Jewish gentleman who dispenses aspirins for everything from the spiritual blues to self-indulgent hangovers, what then can the words of the hymn mean?

> The Son of God goes forth to war,
> A kingly crown to gain;
> His blood-red banner streams afar;
> Who follows in His train?

The Biblical picture is clear enough: "Do not think that I have come to bring peace on earth; I have not come to bring peace, but a sword."

Paul spoke of total conflict between the armies of Christ and the entrenchment of evil: "For though we live in the world we are not carrying on a worldly war, for the weapons of our warfare are not worldly but have divine power to destroy strongholds." The Book of Acts shows us that the strongholds of evil and unbelief are willing to foster every device from riots to bloody persecutions to safeguard their power.

The emissaries of evil are dressed as angels of light, but as a last resort the spirit of sin can be militant and savage. The senses of this generation still have not cleared from witnessing the nightmarish brutality of evil gone to seed. Not very often is the church willing to face the conflict in its realistic dimensions. Bishop Lesslie Newbigin of the Church of South India tells the story of a young Roman Catholic nun who remained in a small town in the Congo in October, 1960, after other whites had fled for their safety. She cried for two days and finally sent a message to her superior, asking, "What do I do?" The reply: "You stay, and if necessary you die." Her crying ceased and her work continued. The bishop asked: "Is that too harsh? It would not be counted so in earthly warfare. Our warfare is not less serious, and a servant is not greater than his Lord."

To say that the church preaching "Christ is Lord" needs courage is to state that the body needs its lifeblood. To say that conformity with the world is a peril to the church is the understatement of all time. Conformity with the enemy is tantamount to total and unconditional surrender. Despite the courageous work of some churches on the spiritual frontiers, as a whole the church has been infiltrated to such an extent that it is doubtful whether God can indefinitely rely on Christ's Body to confront a world dazed by conflict and sick with fear under the shadow of the hydrogen bomb.

The difference between the church of Acts and the church of today is that one was Word-centered and the other is man-centered. For an hour on Sunday morning the Body seems to give the glory to God, but as Professor Gibson Winter points out, "It seems reasonable to assume that approximately one half of the official membership of the churches, possibly as much as two thirds, are religiously tied to an organization rather than personally bound to God or his teachings—a surprising fact in view of the Protestant understanding of faith."

When the condition of the church as a whole was Word-conscious, new men lived in the sphere of the eternal. Heaven, hell, redemption and the Holy Spirit were real. The preaching of the Word was not to save men or to comfort Christians, although those were vital results. The Word was then, and is now, the catalyst of history. By it men were judged and God moved in history. Upon hearing it, men either ran to Christ or stoned the Apostles. The Word still shines in the dark world, and when it is honored as the Word of God, sin is judged, pardon is offered, peace becomes appealing, minds are shaken, hearts are revealed, events are interpreted, the future is foreseen, personal defenses are hardened or weakened, and the spiritual conflict underlying history is intensified. History must lead to the victory of God.

When the Word is hindered, diluted or muffled, we have the intolerable spiritual impasse and morbid frustration that cause the viewing world to be cynical, and that smother the vitalities of the local congregation. Dr. Marion A. Boggs, moderator of the Presbyterian Church in the United States, said in his report at the 1961 General Assembly: "The besetting sin of Presbyterians is complacency. We have a great system of doctrine and a noble form of church government, both of which are grounded in the Holy Scriptures and tested in the crucible of Christian history, but all too many Presbyterians are complacent about it. The sober truth is that we have not yet been able to move the solid mass of our church's membership toward evangelism or toward the missionary outreach of the gospel, or toward any other great objective of Christ's cause and kingdom. . . ."

Our stores and libraries are filled with volumes analyzing the condition of the church. Bishop James A. Pike of the Protestant Episcopal Diocese of California delivered an address at the San Francisco Assembly of the National Council of Churches in which he summarized the basic problems. He mentioned the falling of the church into the institutional ways of prestige-seeking. "In a relatively stable situation they [the members] want to make the church a club for people of 'their sort' rather than a division in the army of the Lord."

Then again, the church has not been true to its message. The church is "at peace with society." Bishop Pike spoke of the man-centered condition of the Body. Finally, he showed that the clergy often live in an atmosphere of fear. They have muffled the message.

Malcolm Boyd states: "And the clergy have turned into 'professionals' like any others, locked in their upper-middle-class stratum of society, and too often conforming to that society. The lack of clerical courage accompanies the increase in clerical worldly security, status, and miscellaneous compensations."

Norman Cousins puts it this way: "The enemy is any man in the pulpit who by his words and acts encourages his congregation to believe that the main purpose of the church or the synagogue is to provide social respectability for its members."

It is not enough to say that neurosis is in the church because it is filled with neurotic persons. There are neurotics in every walk of life. The life of the church is far too complex for superficial analysis. The history of the church must be read to trace present man-centered trends. The church conforms to the world and takes into itself neurotic patterns in which neurotic persons attempt to establish their defenses as realities. These conditions further confuse a man-centered church, producing further illnesses.

Possibly our troubles began when the authority of the Word was undermined by destructive Biblical criticism. Possibly we are not interpreting ourselves correctly when we say there is very little difference between the ministry and the laity, and that if we follow the New Testament we will begin placing the laity in the ministry. Possibly the root cause is to be found in the modern temper that stultified the glorious atoning death and resurrection of our Lord by which lost men receive pardon and sonship from the hand of the eternal Creator. Possibly it is our confusion over the purpose of client-centered psychology in the pastor's practices and theology. The minister comes to feel he must simply stand by the Lord's people while they hit spontaneously on any conclusion in life and theology which gives them the most relief and comfort—whether or not it happens to be sound according to the absolute standards of the Word of God. Possibly in the midst of our fears we are like the Apostles who fled to the refuge of status-seeking, and inquired of the Lord if they might sit with Him in the highest positions of the Kingdom. Possibly by conforming to the world instead of being transformed we took into our community of faith the social and political cleavages that deny faith. Possibly so much of the visible church has become part of the world that when we speak of the church we should be analyzing cell groups and cottage prayer meetings here and there.

Probably we are nearest the truth when we say that it is not one of these causes but many. At any rate, we are on the right track when we say that the greatest threat to the world can not be the world broken before itself, but the church broken before the world.

Ironically enough, our western culture has been most influenced by the Judeo-Christian tradition. The Pharisees raised perfection to a cult, and Jesus stated that true righteousness had to exceed the righteousness of the scribes and Pharisees. Our distorted culture makes a fetish of such idols as perfection of beauty and talent, and it worships status, superiority of prestige and the lofty heights of money-power. When the church adapts to a righteous-coated paganism, the line between church and world becomes increasingly hazy. In the church now, superiority of moral perfection, beauty, talent, brains and an urbane personality are raised to a

·20·

sanctified position of reverence where the neurotic personality is emulated, not treated; he is given praise instead of therapy. Out of this grows further disease, so that while numerous members mimic the world at its own game, some find the unhealthy climate conducive to the expression of their full-blown neurotic personality structure. Several such persons succeed in toiling endlessly to gain control of the program, methods and policies of the church. When this occurs we know there is neurosis in the church. Whole churches can be as ill as any one individual. Any denominational executive can recount the number of churches that are near splitting, or are almost immobile, or have cliques strongly desirous of pushing the minister out.

It would be completely erroneous to assume that church sickness is *always* due to the undermining of the authority of the Word. The truth is that there is as much, if not more, of this illness in fundamentalist churches as in liberal ones. Whatever he professes, the neurotic personality has no creed except the self-imposed, defensive and impossible standards of his own unconscious mind. Partially, these are introjections of the beliefs and standards of his church. Partially, they are distortions of them into the fabric of his own glorified image of himself. Partially, he may react against basic tenets of his church while outwardly adhering to them for self-acceptance. In some cases the strict fundamentalism of his church may act as a disguise for his personal renunciation of the competing world which was too much for him to cope with behind the facade of his own intolerable demands. Each case must be considered separately. The neurotic may have sufficient knowledge of himself to be in vital healing touch with the Holy Spirit. Or he may not. The task of psycho-therapy is to work with the Holy Spirit in reconciling the person with his true and spontaneous being so that he may with full and healthy awareness open his heart and mind to the creative will of God.

Once a church can be ascertained as a sick body, it lives on borrowed time. While it is becoming sick, congregational affairs may appear to run smoothly. Usually it is not until the minister's successor comes to the field and enters into conflict with the controlling neurotic personalities that the deeply rooted symptoms burst into view. The possibility for effective, evangelistic and efficient mission is then remote.

The insular introversion of Protestant churches has ill prepared the clergy for the impossible dilemma of sick churches. Today the priesthood of believers has come to be understood as a theological term for religious democracy. Since the sixteenth century one of Protestantism's major pitfalls—and it may prove to be its greatest—has been the determination of the middle class that their religious life, supported by their purse, will be self-reflecting and self-controlled. Left to its own tendencies, the local church—without the autocratic efficiency of the Roman Catholic Church on one hand, or the controlling authority of the Holy Spirit through the Word honored by deeply consecrated lay and clerical leadership on the other—tends to become ingrown, provincial, and imitative of the economic and cultural prestige-strata of the prevailing community. When this occurs, far from engaging in conflict with the spirit of the world, the church struggles to outdo it in mimicking its neurotic patterns of security. The result is that the task of the clergy changes radically. No longer is the pastor the channel for the Word in preaching, teaching, guidance, challenge and comfort. He now becomes —well, what? Seminaries are not sure.

The seminaries seem to be confused concerning the clerical role. Is the minister to stand by as glorified church manager while the children of God work out their own salvation through a wild flurry of noisy organizational activism? Is he to direct the many affairs of the congregation through committees in such a way that he gets in a good word for God now and then? Is he to be a coach with a fatherly hand for the players? Is he to leave the direction of the clubs and societies to the laymen while he concentrates on counseling and studying for his sermons? Is he to abandon any hope of redeeming the noise and confusion while he prayerfully cultivates small groups and early morning meetings? A good deal of thought is going into the analysis of the nature of the ministry according to the demands of the Bible and the requirements of our modern tempo.

There are, to be sure, countless Protestant pastors—though it is our belief their number is decreasing—who are submissive to the full impact of God's Holy Word, and are trenchantly equipping the saints for the work of the ministry while slowly abandoning the grinding gears of organization which glorify the talents, education and secular initiative of the middle class. There are some souls in the pews who would not tolerate it if their deeply dedicated pastor did not lead them to the battle lines of vested economic interests, political responsibility, racial segregation, community sin and personal holiness. They have come to expect their pastor to call them to a living and dynamic faith in Christ Jesus as Lord and Saviour. Such bodies do not at present characterize Protestantism.

The church pulpit-nominating committees seem to be confused about the clerical role. One pastor who mentioned the importance of evangelism was rejected by a committee on the grounds that the church did not care for fanaticism. Another pastor, with deeply neurotic trends, stayed a short time in several churches but had little trouble in being called to thriving churches. As one woman commented to the committee, "He looks so like a minister. His shoes are shined and he looks like he stepped out of a bandbox. He would cut a fine figure in representing *our* church."

It is certain that introverted churches want a man who can be absorbed into the sea of affability and gooey good will that characterize many churches in general and soaring suburban churches in particular. And certainly the pastors are confused over their roles. Samuel W. Blizzard, professor of Christianity and Society at Princeton Theological Seminary, speaks of the pastor's "master role." This means his concept of the ministry "as an occupation distinguished from the occupational role of other persons." Dr. Blizzard states that the pastor forms an image of how to be effective and successful in his profession partly through his ideology, partly through his experience in the local church, but also, among other spheres, through his relationship to denominational boards, other professions, secular groups, social status in the community, and images derived from experience with other pastors and churches. The minister is under pressure from many sources, and his people see what other ministers are doing in their churches.

If the church has become an institution or a club for the preservation of social identity in the community, then the task of the pastor is confused. He comes to realize that central authority and harmony issuing from binding purpose are hard to find. He may be likened to a politician who has just won an election and is thrown to his little domain with uncertain backing and an ill-defined contract. He must win friends and marshal his forces. He must gain the confidence of the people and come to terms with the powers that be. While he seeks to become a consecrated instrument for the love of Christ, he must also make love and public recognition a policy and method before dinners, family nights, banquets, committees and board meetings. The worst mistake he can make is to look the slightest bit angry for any reason whatever.

Above all, he had better begin producing results. The church up the street is building already, others are renovating. Money should be coming in much faster now. An outstanding program must be kept running to attract members from a wide radius so that there will be no need to minister to undesirable elements in the community who are personally unreliable and economically undependable. The pastor should be a spiritual man and above reproach, but he had better produce big things while he is at it. No wonder that many a pastor feels he had better give first thought to administration and keep on the right side of important persons in the congregation. He may feel he must, but he is obviously not happy about it. In a recent study by the Ministers Life and Casualty Union, it was found that fifty-two per cent of the pastors interviewed were grieved that disproportionately large demands were made upon them by the administrative work of their churches.

"The larger the church, the greater the gripe. In churches with budgets of $19,000 and over and with memberships of 500 and beyond, 58 per cent of the ministers expressed dissatisfaction with the fact that they were too deeply involved in administering the detailed activities of their parishes. Involvement in social activities, administrative details, budgetary matters and the like tend to dull the cutting edge of the minister's spiritual and intellectual impact upon his congregation. Even while expecting and demanding more of the minister's time for these affairs, the average parish is quick to sense and to complain of the decline in his spiritual stature as a consequence of his having to spend so much time in running the church's machinery."

We must note that the particular creed one adheres to is

not a major factor in determining the relative merits of being a successful pastor and being an effective one. Dr. Blizzard says, "Ministers holding different concepts of the theological dimension of their master role do not differ from one another with respect to their concept of effectiveness and success."

When Dr. Blizzard speaks of the "lack of relationship between the minister's ideological perspective about himself and his working norms," he is probably providing the clue to the study of those conflicts that result in the pastor breaking down or leaving his work for a secular position. It is a frightening thing for a minister to realize that he may be divorced from his true center of being. No longer can he think of himself as a healing servant in the image of Christ, but as a headwaiter in an endless round of luncheons. No longer is he to think of himself as the leader of a charging brigade, but as a four-star general among a brigade of three-star generals. His task is to hold the fort and build morale while dress parades are undertaken with zeal and fervor. Should he antagonize the wrong officials he may discover he is really an orderly in a company of high brass, and not an officer at all. As a human being with prestige, success, finances, future and family to think of, the minister, in the face of terribly increasing demands on his time and strength from his congregation and his own conscience, must ask the same question of both His Lord and his official board: "How am I doing?"

Every shepherd knows that his may be a calling that leads to tears and persecution, and the cross he bears for God's people is the cross of His Master. But there is something dreadfully and radically wrong with Protestantism when the pastor is chained to a sick church. All the while he seeks to appease the forces of neuroticism through the attitude of submissiveness and the ministrations of love, he somehow senses that he is only sinking deeper into the mire.

The prophet caught between conflicting demands usually senses that until such time as radical changes are made in denominational and church administration, and until new concepts of the pastor's function are brought to bear on the congregation, he must gently lead the people who so desire in their commitment to Christ and His service. At the same time he is usually forced to adjust to the social dynamics of the situation he inherited from the previous pastor. He struggles at all costs to avoid the path of expediency, but he is aware of the current thinking. His function must alternate between a fatherly master of ceremonies and a saccharine funeral director. When anything goes wrong he must automatically take a good deal of the blame. He must be the instrument for the recognition of prestige and achievement in every religious VIP. He will be well advised to compliment children and parents alike, and be especially cordial to members who have freely given many years of service to the choir. Invitations to cultural meetings held in the church are to be accepted, and certainly when the invitation is extended by friends or relatives of prominent members of the official boards. No matter what the situation, the pastor must be ready to wear a painted smile to demonstrate God's happiness with everyone.

Many of the remedies glibly offered in popular magazines and books for the minister often fail to appreciate his anxiety. The advice, "Learn to say no," and "Don't wear yourself out hopping to every social event in church," fails to comprehend his fear that the ire of a disgruntled layman may do far more damage than a fatiguing schedule. Let others start a Let's-Learn-to-Say-No movement. Most ministers do not feel ready for such interesting innovations.

The pastor has no trouble putting his finger on those persons in the parish who are charging subsurface tensions.

He tries to keep fires from breaking out elsewhere because the spot that always smolders may suddenly burst into an inferno. It is almost too much to hope that in the modern church one problem will arise at one time. "There are so many conditions in the ministry that tend to make us loveless: stubbornness, obstinate church councils, alcoholics, neurotics, bosses in the church, pettiness, lack of cooperation (the capable refuse, the inept volunteer), choirs."

The modern pastor leaps at signs of personal victory here and there among his people, and lives as best he can with his conscience while he evaluates the flurries of aimless energy in the congregation as a whole. He is sure that only the power and love of the Holy Spirit enable him to rise above the futility of unceasing activism that goes under the name of religion, while he seeks to lead precious souls into new fields of exciting endeavor for Christ. His enemy before the world is conformity. In the church it is also defeatism. He is regretful that his hands are tied by the failures of modern Protestantism and that a few persons are able to prevent him from performing on a whole-church scale what he is doing here and there for individuals and cell groups.

If the pastor has just been ordained, he probably goes to a small church that has witnessed the circulation of many members while the most influential, and often the most neurotic, persons remain for years. It is not likely that the young, courageous prophet of the Lord will encounter a breathless expectancy with his vow to preach and teach the whole counsel of God without fear or favor. If he will not find this expectancy in the small, inner-city charge, or in the rich, downtown church, or in the 200-500-member church in the transitional neighborhood—and he certainly will not find it in the self-conscious, insular, suburban church—where then can he turn?

It is neither sincere nor realistic to ignore the spiritual condition of Protestantism, and the many sick churches it has fathered, by giving pious-sounding and irrelevant advice to burdened ministers. Such an attitude is no service to our Lord. Of course pastors are required to rely patiently, not on their own efforts, but on the supernatural work of the Holy Spirit. When was that not true for any lasting accomplishment in the name of God? Now and then ministers write to religious psychiatrists or counseling experts, and deep understanding and spiritual counsel are provided. At other times, a nebulous mixture of psychology and religion is offered up in labored sentences, sufficiently expert-sounding to cause guilt in the reader, but not clear or practical enough to be useful.

Our need is clear. It is to come to grips with the spiritual condition of Protestantism in general. Then we must be realistic about the dynamics of the neurotic church. A clear diagnosis must precede therapy by the Holy Spirit at a time when the church must minister with full efficiency and power to a world desperately in need of God.

2

Organism
and Organization

THE PASTOR RAPS THE EDGE OF THE PULPIT SHARPLY WITH his knuckles and declares strongly: "The church is not society's organization. It is God's organism!" By this he means that the church is to have no life, structure and purpose of her own self-asserting continuity apart from the ongoing ministry of her Head and reigning Lord, Christ Jesus. As Christ is the incarnation of the Father, so the church is the incarnation of the Holy Spirit ministering through the interaction of persons whose overriding purpose in life is to be the tongue, the hands, the feet, the flesh and blood of the risen Saviour. The heartbeat of Christ's Body is the love of God. Her mind is the mind of Christ. As the uplifted hand can not disobey the command of the brain to rise, neither can the church refuse to raise outstretched hands of invitation in response to the compassion of her one Lord.

Somewhere along the line, an excuse was offered in the terms "invisible and visible" to soften the departure of the church from this mission. Unfortunately, the true church is too often invisible indeed! The visible church has, in fact, been institutionalized and, for the most part, is adhering to the social laws and predictions defined by the social sciences. The neurotic personality in the churches must be understood as drawing upon and subscribing to basic prevailing elements in our culture and in institutionalized churches. It was inevitable that some elements of the institutionalizing process

would preserve the churches in varying communities and in different ages. It comes as a shock, however, to realize that the Protestant bodies which stressed the role of the laity have now absorbed so much of the values and practices of the surrounding worldly culture. The church is now the pious cultural altar, sanctifying the prevailing security values of pride and prestige. It becomes the self-conscious reflection of station in life as determined by non-Christian elements of society. In numerous cases that we shall later examine it becomes the vehicle of compensating for a false sense of security, through pride and prestige, that was never quite attained in the outside cultural or economic spheres.

Now the church may be studied, not against the background of the Book of Acts, but in the realm of the social sciences. The churches as an institution are a closely knit group of social usages. The institution in general, "once established, tends to unify its component elements and also to adjust itself as a unit to the total cultural system of its society."

Modes of belief and folkways are not institutionalized until they have been completely adopted. Symbols tend to give them permanence and stability. Adaptations to changes in society are slow indeed, and are often militantly resisted. All institutions have oral or written traditions that do not change over the years. Behavior patterns are prescribed and deviation is frowned upon. Institutions meet rather specific needs, and some churches prefer talking in tongues, handclapping and spontaneous demonstrations of the Spirit. Other behavior patterns within the institution are catholic in nature, meeting more general needs. Thus, almost all churches have a cross somewhere, and the people close their eyes in prayer, etc.

Institutions are means of deriving and maintaining status.

They issue certificates, bestow honors and observe certain rites for those who stoutly maintain basic purposes and strictly follow the ground rules. The group breathes a deeper feeling of security when it honors those who have preserved the solidarity and identity of the whole.

The church as institution has a unifying effect, making for wholeness of the individual in a revolutionary world. He is, first of all, united to all men everywhere who believe and act as he does. His denomination boasts so many million members in America alone, many more around the world. Those who bring in more members are rewarded with augmented standing. Those responsible for members leaving or becoming disturbed are punished.

Second, the individual is united to the ages. Five hundred years ago man believed and behaved in church as he does now. Truth is absolute. Holding it gives him security and comfort. God is immutable. Change and decay are all around us, but God who changes not will abide with us.

Third, he is united to the continuing best elements in himself. It was before the holy altar that his parents professed their faith, that he was baptized, that he consecrated himself to eternal truth and goodness, that he was married, and before which he will baptize his own children. The world may topple around him, but before that altar he prays to the Rock of Ages. New civilizations on other planets may rise and dwarf the cosmic significance of earth, but in the same pew Sunday after Sunday this man worships Christ, the same yesterday, today and forever.

No wonder that a pastor so frequently hears the outcry, "But we never did *that* before in *this* church!" Change and disorder in the church are encountered with holy hostility. "Because churches rarely venture out of the middle of the road, controversy and disagreement are not usually provoked

by great social questions. Disagreements over budgets, choirs, or who uses the church building frequently pre-empt debate, decision, and action on the great issues of our time."

One might expect, after reading Acts, that the church would be regarded with caution, or respect, or outright antagonism for continually upsetting the world's conscience. Actually, the opposite is true. Far from being a militant Body subject to the authority of the written and living Word, the churches wait off to the sidelines to see how the dust will settle after social revolution. They can bestow their blessings on those apparently stable and victorious elements that emerge after the struggle. They may even accept these elements into their midst. Thus, the church, instead of going forth as the harbinger of change wrought by the Holy Spirit, sees its function as the sanctifying institution to bless what appears to be final and enduring. If, for example, the integration of the races ever becomes an established fact throughout America, many churches will eventually make some provisions in recognition of that fact. Belatedly they may even place some Negroes on official boards if failure to do so would incur the disapprobation of the surrounding culture.

In the meantime, change within the institution is precisely what most Christians do not want to witness. "Such change is bewildering and frightening. We feel the need for some institutions that do not change or that at least provide orderly continuity and stability. It is no wonder that many people want the church to be such an institution. . . . If these people have been trained by the church itself to think of it as primarily the conservator of social tradition and the source of personal comfort, they can be expected to take the position that it should mind its own business and not get mixed up in desegregation. If it does so, it increases their tension and discomfort."

The rigidity of the church not only provides for many a sense of God's immutability, but His transcendence as well. The congregational life goes on above the maelstrom of world events, much as the sun is high above the shreds of human dignity floating amid the flotsam and jetsam of social chaos. Who cares how matters turn out? The victors will have to come to terms with God anyway—and that is true enough.

Then there is God's grace. The ancient means of providing rank and status not only make for a sense of security today, but they effuse a glow of God's graciousness toward His righteous ones. It becomes the task of the clergy—each minister an official symbol of the divine order of the total church—to speak for the congregation and for God in bestowing rank and rewarding with prestige.

In a number of cultures the concepts of status, according to church and community, differ. Here the tenacious maintenance of the truth and the old ways may be a prophetic judgment against society. Every time the Baptist Church of Moscow, U.S.S.R., conducts worship according to the old traditions by which Christ is adored in Word and sacrament, it is a public protest against the Communist worship of antichrist.

When institutions clash there is a tendency for one of them to give ground or accommodate to the other. If not, persons can unconsciously change behavior to suit the requirements of the job, lodge, community club, union, and the monthly meeting of the board of deacons. It never dawns on these Christians that they have erected an impregnable wall in the unconscious between the golf course and the sanctuary. Personal comfort and peace of mind prefer that institutions act in harmony with overlapping folkways. Many Christians have taken the injunction "to bring the world into harmony with the will of Christ" to mean that the church should be brought into the world, not for reconciliation but for accommodation.

Our true task is coming into focus with increasing clarity. The problem is to infiltrate all areas of life with the zeal of Christian vocation, without adapting to the sub-Christian patterns of society. The community of God is not gaining in the solution of this problem to the degree we should expect if she were committed mind, heart and body to her primal goal. To the world—and here we are speaking of the secular culture of America in particular—the Christian thrust has the impact of a creampuff and is tasted occasionally as such a delicacy. "In a world looking for the new, the Church tells the old, old story. Some people are bored with it. The churches themselves suspect that it does not exactly fit our world. They try timid or desperate schemes to refurbish it. Sometimes they forget the important fact that it never did exactly fit this world."

The churches have had a palpable effect on the outward morals of society, so that sin is something to be opposed as a public policy and God's backing is good to have for the success of anything worth while. The result of this mutual patronage is that the church as an institution can conform to the neighborhood's standards to receive its approbation while bestowing rank on solid citizens in a manner acceptable to the neighborhood.

Both the church and the community agree that status will be bestowed in the church on the righteous ones. In fact, character should be flawless—in public, of course. The holier the better, but no fanaticism, please. In addition, success still is nothing to be sneezed at in the most prosperous nation in the world. The superintendent of the church school, the steward, the trustee, the elder, the deacon, the president of the men's association and the lay representative to synod ought to be solid citizens in some economic echelon generally monopolized by their particular denomination, with executives pretty well covered by the Presbyterians and Episcopalians. If he has a lowly job during the week, a man stands a chance—in some churches—of compensating in a vital church position, provided he is not obnoxious, can quietly command respect, and has labored hard and long to strengthen the church in prestige, self-respect, stewardship, successful programs, or in numbers. While Jesus seemed to have something to do with sinners, it is generally recognized now that there must be no breath of scandal, past or present, associated with anyone who intends to amount to something in church.

It is also generally recognized that the churches will reward those who have made the grade financially in society, no matter how pagan that society may be.

▣ ▣ ▣

Mr. Smith, vice-president in charge of sales for Dixmuth Manufacturing Co., moved into fashionable Greenview Heights with his wife and three darling children. One evening he was visited by Deacons Ryan (office manager) and Bryan (attorney). Both officers were deeply respected for their evangelistic concern. One or two remarks were once passed that they were a bit too religious, but on the whole they were respected for their statements that a good church should "witness."

Both men informed Mr. Smith that the people who amounted to something in Greenview Heights were quite at home at the Greenview Community Church. There was another church on the south side, closer to Big City, and everyone was only too glad to see more of the laboring class go there to worship among their own kind. Folks should feel at home where they worship, right? And the preacher at Greenview Community was known state-wide as one of the most congenial after-dinner speakers and humorists the folks ever heard, and no kidding about that!

But don't think the church isn't democratic! Why the board of trustees has a carpenter on it! Father and mother have been going to the church for twenty-five years. The deacons have a machinist, but you'd never know him by the spiffy way he dresses. His father was an elder in Philadelphia.

So you can see it is a truly Christian church, where the folks are so "old shoe" that the fellow next to you might be the president of some big firm and you'd never even know it. It was agreed by the visitors and Mr. Smith that the new family would be happier among folks where their talents and gracious personalities would be put to most effective use in the Kingdom.

▣ ▣ ▣

One is not quite sure what turn the witnessing would have taken if, after a half-hour friendly visit, Mr. Smith turned out to be a grease monkey who had saved his money for twenty years. If he had then met basic qualifications and was determined to acquire status, after quite a few years there would be no general objection to his serving the Lord on, say, the cabinet of the men's guild or on the board of deacons.

"One can be *in* grease and not *of* it, and this is characteristically true of church members in the major denominations who are recruited from the blue-collar ranks. One way in which the major denominations have mirrored the economic ladder is by recruiting almost exclusively from the middle classes and welcoming those from the blue-collar ranks whose hearts were set on things above."

The role of the pastor in this case is clear. It is to recognize and authenticate in the name of God the orders of prestige. After all, how much more can you hope for if you have the prestige that comes from God? The minister is the mouthpiece of God and the congregation in recognizing rank and status in those churches in which the institutionalizing process has proceeded unhindered.

The task of oiling the organizational wheels to work in harmony so that leaders may lead and followers may follow in peace takes up from thirty to fifty per cent of the minister's time. The chances of changing this situation are so dim that the minister is now known as the "pastoral director." Keeping all forces and parties in peace and balance is no easy task. The pastor knows that his service to the "powers that be" determines how long he will stay at his job. These little tasks include such items as:

1) Put notice in the bulletin that this is the sixth consecutive term Mrs. Jones is serving "officially" on the board of the Ladies' Aid.

2) See that the birth of little Smith boy, 8¼ pounds, son of the cousin of the chairman of the official board, is prominently displayed on the bulletin board and put in the weekly printed announcements.

3) Recognize, at a service of dedication, Mrs. Beardsly, who has two sons in the ministry and whose uncle is celebrating his twentieth year on the mission field. (After a while the pastor acquires the skill of picking up such information—somehow.)

4) Write a letter of appreciation to steward Jones for his extremely skillful and dedicated leadership of the Parlor Renovation Campaign, to be written respectfully in longhand and read by the associate pastor at the board meeting and morning service.

5) At all banquets and very important functions—particularly where guests are present—have the Divine Order stand with wives and husbands in order of rank, beginning with the official board down. One is always a bit nervous after these recognitions in fear that someone has been neglected.

It is usually assumed by fellow pastors that their colleagues seek out small suburban churches about to burst into thousand-member beehives, because of their similarity to a get-rich-quick tip in real estate. Actually the chief attractive feature appears to be the opportunity for the new minister to build his own governing power structure around himself.

Contrast this with a pastor's installation into an old established church where the hierarchy is inherited. If the previous minister exercised little direct administration because of masochistic or rather extreme self-abnegating tendencies, and if he depended upon certain prominent individuals to do most of his pastoral directing for him, then almost nothing can be done by the succeeding minister in the field of incisive spiritual venture. It is a rare church in the heart of the city that is doing anything vital or relevant for Christ and the community unless the pastor started with a few remaining members or the denomination undertook an inner-city work in conjunction with other churches. If the pastor has a church of two to six hundred in the city, and it is at least twenty years old, in almost all cases in American Protestantism as it is today he must spend half his time smiling and oiling the machine furiously while trusting that his vital and enduring work for Christ will be in the souls of men here and there who discover spiritual resources at the crossroads of opportunity and crisis.

Once the community of the Spirit has been hardened into a brittle mirror of the world's system of pride, there is not much for the minister to do but continue the process with as much piety as his conscience can muster and as much vision as the people will allow. As we shall presently see, out of this environment a Pandora's box of neuroses has opened to flood us with symptoms giving rise in turn to more ills. But we may well ponder for a moment how it is we live in a world where black can slowly become white and still be called black, and where the church can become part of the world and still be called the church.

Possibly we are lulled into a false sense of satisfaction because the churches are busy. What on earth is busier than a church today? No one but the pastor knows everything that is going on. There are committees and banquets, and committees to co-ordinate committees, and lunches to prepare. And who is busier than a minister? They well understand William Gannett's phrase, "Blessed be drudgery!" In their long hours, dedicated shepherds are ministering, caring, understanding, listening, encouraging, studying, thinking and praying. In counseling they share the intimate secrets of blighted hearts for hour after hour. The paths they take with fellow sinners to Calvary's cross are well trod, and they share the joy of compassionate lay brethren in beholding anew the mysteries of redemption from sin and a thousand sicknesses of the soul. And who are more like the best ministers we have seen than those saints who make life dear to us because they love and share so openly, and so clearly remind us of Christ?

But perhaps we are also saddened when we think of these saints, because most pastors are utterly sincere, and because churches are busy and God's laborers dream dreams of salvation for a war-frightened world. How can we be the conservators of the saints' golden deeds if our responses to today's challenges are fragmentary and scattered?

We must slowly shake our heads in wonder when we read again the New Testament and see how the problems that arose from pride then were not very different from those today. Fears and status-climbing infiltrated the early church. James was surprised that the church gave such preference to the rich, and Paul reminded Christians that God shows no partiality. The Apostle did attempt to keep a fine balance. On the one hand he appealed to a good sense of pride, if you will, by paying his churches well-deserved compliments. But lest they become puffed up he reminded them: "For consider your call, brethren; not many of you were wise according to worldly standards, not many were powerful, not many were of noble birth; but God chose what is foolish in the world to shame the wise, God chose what is weak in the world to shame the strong, God chose what is low and despised in the world, even things that are not, to bring to nothing things that are, so that no human being might boast in the presence of God."

It is a matter of conjecture whether the Jerusalem church failed to live up to its promise of becoming the leading spiritual congregation because of its pride in race, location and leadership. At any rate, leadership passed to the Gentile churches, while the stars of others waned. We do not need to look afar to see the church of Laodicea.

Dr. G. Campbell Morgan wrote an excellent comment on Acts 19. You will remember that in the Biblical account Demetrius was intensely hostile because Paul's preaching of the gospel had ruined his business which catered to idolatry and superstition. A mob scene ensued. The town clerk quieted the crowd, and the mob desisted. Writes Dr. Morgan: "I do not criticize the King or Court for receiving; but I do say that the Church of God is in her gravest peril when a town clerk protects her. Let us be very careful that we do not waste our energy, and miss the meaning of our high calling, by any rejoicing in the patronage of the world. It is by the friction of persecution that the fine gold of character is made to flash and gleam with glory. The Church persecuted has always been the Church pure, and therefore the Church powerful. The Church patronized has always been the Church in peril, and very often the Church paralyzed. I am not afraid of Demetrius. Let him have his meeting of craftsmen, and let them in their unutterable folly shout a lie twenty-five thousand strong. The truth goes quietly on. But when the town clerk begins to take care of us, then God deliver us from the peril."

In numerous Protestant churches in America, Acts 19 has taken a new turn. The church accommodated herself sufficiently to welcome Demetrius into membership (with a little cleaning up on his part), and the town clerk is now on the session.

When the believing community plays house with herself and the workings of her group relationships are motivated by the same dynamics as the Community Bell-Ringers For a Prettier Greenview Heights, then those who lust most for superiority, power, pride and prestige will find they have the qualifications to make a successful go of it in almost any introverted church. After all, the congregation does appear to have one distinct advantage: the reflected prestige of God.

However we manage to retrace our steps, undo the wrong, do what has been undone, and return to the fellowship of Christ's death and resurrection, we will have to deal with the obstacles and confusions resulting from the work of the neurotic personality in the Protestant Church. To an analysis of this personality and to the symptoms of a sick church we now turn our attention.

3
Tyranny of the Idols

LET US MAKE A FRESH REVIEW OF BASIC FACTORS UNDERLYING the neurotic's religious concepts and his church-related activities. The various functions of neurotic symptoms could be observed from many vantage points. Let us choose the one with which the Bible is most familiar: idolatry.

The growing child must cope with the urge of the core of his true being for self-realization. A self-concept, or self-image, develops as this urge is fulfilled in the fires of conflicting emotions. Innate resources and talents are molded within the limits imposed by parents and society. Parents may encourage the child's concepts of his own loveworthiness and dependability. If the child is accepted and loved for himself, he learns to give love despite any hardships, disappointments or physical handicaps.

Parents or surrogates may, in other cases, "use" the child, expecting him to surpass his playmates in intellectual achievements, or to outdo other children in displays of affection and affability. He may be taught to have no feelings or desires except those that have passed parental approval, or he may be taunted to evince superior ruggedness and a fiercely competitive spirit. There may be several dominant and contradictory sides to his nature. He may be obsequious before bullies, only to turn into a bully himself among those he considers weaker than himself.

As the self-image forms, it reflects what a human being feels about himself: either he thinks of himself as a good-looking person with many fine qualities, or as a foolish-looking, inept specimen who could never make the grade. His image also reflects anticipations and aspirations: "With my liabilities, I'll never make good," or, "People appreciate the talents and disposition I have." This self-image includes a person's relationship with others: "When people get to know me, they usually like me," or, "I hate to have people know me well, because then they drop me. It is better to keep some distance from people. Familiarity breeds contempt."

Before mention is made of neurotic solutions, consider the idolatry of the immature personality. As a reflection of self, his idol is as rigid and unrealistic as a totem pole, and often carries as many faces. He may worship beauty, race, money, freedom, an escapist ideal, or superior intellectual beauty. The alcoholic for awhile may be pleased that he worships the great god Freedom. In all cases it becomes important to locate fellow worshipers of the same idol, or else the idolatry is meaningless. The cult of beauty and sex appeal can attract more devotees to Hollywood and Vine than to the nursing profession.

The stage on which the idol sits is called Pride, and each soul has a great stake in his particular idol. He has or hopes to have the qualities or the wealth that appeal to fellow members of the cult. If the idol is swept away by disappointment or disaster, pride is shattered. The crash in the stock market in 1929 brought the fall of major idols, and numerous cultists opened windows and went to their death.

If the gospel of the one true God and the crucifixion of His Son by religious idolators is preached, pride rebels. The discovery that one is worshiping an idol is a confrontation of the self by God. God's Spirit calls, "Adam, where are you?" He answers, "I am naked and alone, and I thought by hiding I could keep that fact from You." The Lord will permit no other gods before Him. Even the mature person discovers that his deepest loves are idolatries unless he has felt the cleansing of soul and God's blessing which the love of Christ applies to the heart.

Idolatry in the neurotic is a different story. Quite often a child cannot cope with the hostile and rejecting attitudes one or both parents may use to make him subservient to their needs. His solutions include the possibilities of falling on them for mercy, running away from all hostile persons, or demonstrating aggression and superiority before threats. One of these trends becomes dominant. More and more the child becomes what he feels he must be to defend himself against a basically unloving, tragedy-ridden and threatening world.

The loss of identity is a cruel and paralyzing blow to human personality. Who is he? What is he looking for in life? How can he be safe, superior, happy and loved (or at least respected)—all at the same time? The answer is clear: to tie together the loose ends of his personality he unconsciously develops an idealized image of himself. Out of the air he pulls a magic wand, and with it he waves into being a person who would shame Apollo by comparison. His idol becomes a rigid, tyrannical, completely unrealistic image of a thoroughly superior, perfect, glamorous, glorious god.

As Alfred Adler asserts, "No human being can bear a feeling of inferiority for long; he will be thrown into a tension which necessitates some kind of action. But suppose an individual is discouraged; suppose he cannot conceive that if he makes realistic efforts he will improve the situation. He will still be unable to bear his feelings of inferiority; he will still struggle to get rid of them; but he will try methods which will bring him no further ahead. His goal is still 'to be superior to difficulties,' but instead of overcoming obstacles he will try to hypnotize himself, or auto-intoxicate himself, into *feeling* superior. Meanwhile his feelings of inferiority will accumulate, because the situation which produces them remains unaltered. The provocation is still there. Every step he takes will lead him further into self-deception, and all his problems will press in upon him with greater and greater urgency."

The imagined person must become the real person until neither he nor anyone else knows any other. It is not simply that he wants to be perfectly righteous; he *is* perfectly righteous. Any suggestion to the contrary is met with incredulity, anxiety, then guilt, then hostility. He sees both power and safety in superiority, and the superior position is buttressed by perfection.

The power striven for is unlimited power. It may be the power of brute force, vindictive triumph over others, intellectual superiority, saintliness, or escapist self-sufficiency. As Adler pointed out, even compliance with one and all, plus utter devotion to love itself, can be an instrument of power over others.

This person is ever alert to protect the idol. The sincere and unwary critic becomes a dangerous enemy to be deceived or defeated. It is somewhat like a children's winter game called "King of the Hill." The little ones scramble up a snowpile and whoever manages to stay on top is king. The others automatically become opponents and any means of holding the throne, short of mayhem, is both legal and clever. The ruler is glorious but lonely. He has no friends who would not love to be up there in his place. The moment he lets down his guard they will charge up from all sides.

This is the neurotic's position. He dreams of himself as being head and shoulders over the mob, and above criticism. During sleep, his unconscious takes over and he may dream of falling from great heights. His acrophobia may be a fear of falling from grace or losing his grandeur. But in waking

·46·

life he must not be aware of making mistakes. Errors (in his way of thinking) are accidents. Hatred is righteous indignation. Lies are clever tricks to outwit Satan. Judgments of another's conduct shows a perspicacious religious spirit. Gossip issues from a holy and sensitive nature. If others do not appreciate his godliness, it only proves their sinfulness.

How can a human being be loving, or saintly and still be superior, rigid and supercilious? Such an untenable position leads to a broad boulevard of frustration. The position is held, nevertheless, and in addition it implies in his mind that those who do not respect it deserve punishment. "For," his reasoning goes, "if I love and serve you, and give you the benefit of my righteous example, and you do not respond by respecting all my wishes, then that only demonstrates your hardness to God's will. Why, you must be a hypocrite!" Claims on humanity are stringent. A deal is made with life whereby superiority places an *a priori* claim on others which they must meet. The neurotic mother may spend half her life sacrificing herself for her children. In return, she feels they owe her the shared glow of their prestige, their service, their children, their time, and whatever else she may desire. If they don't feel the same way, they will be unfair. Neurotic claims frequently cause others to feel guilty for not meeting them.

If the disturbed individual is a type with deep, conflicting trends of compliance, he may be timid about asserting his claims. He thinks, "People are so cruel, blind and suspicious that I must be cautious in showing my superior enlightenment." Needless to say, the intense anger that smolders only causes further intense suffering and resentment. Rationalization is the very spirit of this style of life. Everything else is to blame when the universe does not turn on his private timetable. Everyone else is to blame when they do not step into line.

The neurotic personality is not in touch with his true core of being. Reality must be twisted into any mold required to actualize the ideal image into the ideal self. When he fails to measure up to this glorious vision of self, then his very intention is proof of his lofty being. When true and spontaneous feelings from within him come to the surface, they are suppressed at all costs. No wonder that at times life itself seems weary, distant or even clouded with death. The truth must be avoided because it hurts. He lives only for the assurance that his image is the truth and his idol reigns supreme.

Neurotic pride is the self-assurance that the idolized self is synonymous with reality. But this pride is always attacked, for the world fails to accept forever this kind of person on his own terms. People resent being humiliated, threatened or made to feel guilty. Most other persons are in too close touch with reality to accept as fact a world that is nothing more than a set of mirrors reflecting someone's grandiose fantasies.

When a slip in action occurs, the neurotic feels guilty. The blame must quickly be put on someone or something to ward off hatred against the self. Inner dictates become even more grievous, and an ironclad sense of "rightness" and "wrongness" governs every thought, every act. Extreme pride is invested in this false morality. The neurotic's bearing often becomes affected, cool and rigidly poised. He is deathly afraid of losing his temper and derives a gleeful satisfaction in observing others lose their poise. In any situation, he assumes a pompous and regal responsibility that is sometimes amazing. He is both the center of attention and the one charming authority on what is right and wrong. It is either a great threat or a flat jest if his weighty opinion does not settle a matter immediately. If it is pointed out to him that parts of his life do not demonstrate the epitome of virtue, he quickly shrugs this off. He has a perfect *knowledge* of the right, and is really so godlike that lesser mortals must have their sense of reality impaired if they don't acknowledge it. If, however, he fails openly enough he soon dabbles in his pursuits with a disdainful detachment. Every venture is such a threat that he must force himself to certain tasks such as working, composing, making a speech or leading a discussion. How can the world be so unfair that others get the credit for what was really *his* idea, *his* intention?

☖ ☖ ☖

Mary K. always came to the women's meetings like a fairy queen, smiling gently at all, making a few witty or complimentary remarks to officers and key persons. She never entered fully into any of the activities, although she relished being consulted on important matters. A new president would not be nominated without her prior approval. She never really accepted and followed through on any sustained responsibility in co-ordination with the officers. Finally, she took an office but not much hard work was put into it from week to week. It should have been quite enough that she consented to lend her prestige to the group by her very presence. Several outspoken ladies were heard to remark that she humbly forced herself to take the credit in times of success, but when some venture related to her office failed, it was obvious that she thought associates could not implement her brilliant and progressive plans.

☖ ☖ ☖

If the true core of the neurotic's humanity knocks on his heart's door, its call to self-realization is promptly stifled. He is preoccupied with psychological fence-mending. Defenses are in conflict with themselves, and working out solutions takes continual time and effort. If for example he is the type who yearns for brute, naked power, and is ready to employ subtle but effective tactics of humiliation to achieve it, the wrath and envy of those under his power must be warded off. No matter what he does, they ought to respect him. This is no mean task. How are both sides of the coin going to show at the same time? Somehow the whole conflict must evaporate. Failure to rid himself of any awareness of his own human limitations will incur his resentment of himself as a totally worthless person. Again he lashes himself until his spirit is actually weakened by self-hate. He does not lash himself for being a psychological fraud; he does it because he hates the core of his true being for not measuring up to his picture of the faultless and benevolent king.

This stoical disparagement of the self only serves to show the world a very religious person. He is proud to *be* (not merely appear) selfless. He is glad to accept that reputation in church, and frequently encourages it by wearing a gentle smile for everyone and by telling himself that, outside of a few dangerous hypocrites, he likes people. This masquerade might continue undisturbed were it not for the externalization of his self-hate. Externalization means that a person experiences his inner feelings as if they were caused by outside forces. "There are certain people who envy and despise me", may be another way of saying, "I despise myself." The neurotic personality is a particularly suspicious one, and to preserve the integrity of his pride he must be on the alert to beat his enemies to the first blow. Sudden flare-ups in temper make him lash more vehemently at himself because his halo slipped, and he constricts his feelings more rigidly so there will be no humiliating recurrences. The vicious cycle continues on and on. Year after year the inner tyrannies grow more ruthless. Like Georges Jacques Danton, he makes his way to the guillotine of a vast oblivion, and year after year he mutters, "Danton, no weakness."

Self-abnegation and reaction against enjoyment may continue as forms of self-lashing. Partially, inhibitions may be a strong reaction-formation against emotions the neurotic fears. They may also be expressions of self-hate and an attempt to frustrate all enjoyable initiative which might be a liability in keeping the facade of his godlikeness before the world. Others may remark that so-and-so cares nothing for himself and is completely dedicated to the Kingdom, but little do these observers realize that he has so lost himself that he is often listless, almost indifferent at times to life itself. Real life, real persons and his real self are threatening and obnoxious to him.

The hatred against inward and outward threats brings us to the subject of neurotic vindictiveness. It is our observation that next to nothing constructive in church polity, therapy or administration is being accomplished today toward an understanding of the phenomenon of neurotic vindictiveness. A vindictive nature is one that is bent on retaliation, humiliation of foes, punishment and vengeance. It is a thread sewn into the very fabric of neurosis. The subject could fill volumes and we can touch only briefly on the reasons for it.

First, to be revered the idol must be high above other persons and idols. The idol is raised in proportion to the vindictive triumphs over competing foes. Second, when others criticize the neurotic they punch holes in his dike against an ocean of anxiety. Extreme hate is engendered against those he blames for his anxiety. Third, when someone has injured neurotic pride, the question is not one of getting even. It becomes a matter of obliterating—with an utterly glorious victory—the foe who questioned the supremacy of the idol.

Pride can only be restored by subjecting real or imagined enemies to the most humiliating public fate. Fourth, because of the externalization of self-hate, others are seen as potential allies or enemies. When enemies, they must be dealt with. The more the neurotic lashes himself, the more on guard he is against his foes. Thus, when he strikes, it is with an almost inhumanly subtle ferocity. The mere suggestion that others will not stand being humiliated brings his vindictiveness to a white heat.

The more he falters in his idolatry the more the neurotic person must restore pride, make further absonant claims, experience more frustration and feel increasingly vindictive toward obstacles in his upward road to glory. There is a bottomless pit of retaliatory spirit in him which gets more intense with every passing year. Time does not heal it, friends cannot throw a sop to it, enemies cannot appease it, trusted allies never completely evade it, and life itself is crushed before it. One can readily see how the vindictive soul with contradictory claims for love and/or respect from everyone, on the basis of goodness, humility and service, can be torn in two. Vindictiveness and the need for approval and respect mix like fire and oil. Unhindered, this battle within the soul can lead only to listlessness or illness at best, catastrophic breakdown at worst.

Needless to say, life cannot continue for long when it is torn by indiscriminate forces of self-destruction. Neither can anyone continue forever in hostility toward the whole world for not joyfully authenticating neurotic claims for superiority. Integrating the personality into one cohesive whole becomes an upward grind, to say the very least. The search for wholeness is really a desire to eliminate anomalies in conduct so that the facade will be one of force, perfection and self-sufficiency. In the case of the compliant and self-effacing neurotic type, the weakness to be avoided is anything deviating from love and service.

There are periods in which the neurotic's whole psyche is taken up with the urge to be vindictive. He despises in others the weaknesses, sentiment and gentleness he will not tolerate in himself. But he must admit that he needs others to validate his exorbitant demands. Often he develops what we call a "negative set" toward one person or group. The target of his wrath becomes his scapegoat and Public Enemy No. 1. He imagines that this target is the entire cause of his unhappiness and his need for vindictiveness, and he relates all wrongs to one enemy who no longer can do anything but more wrong. Thus, the "negative set" means that all vindictiveness is channeled against one target in the hope that public triumph over him will bolster the neurotic's pride, justify his feelings of hostility, and strengthen his faltering search for grandeur.

▣ ▣ ▣

Mr. William K. had been Sunday school superintendent for twenty years. Not much progress had been made in methods, administration or attendance, but Mr. K. reveled in leading a long opening service complete with sermon and endless announcements. Some observers remarked that he reminded them of a frustrated minister. This position was his whole life in the church, and suggestions for improving classes or worship were met with tolerant smiles or a withering stare. Perfection and service in this area entitled him to direct the pastor, officers and prominent members. When he rose to speak at congregational meetings, it was with a flourish of fatherly imperiousness, as if the last word on the subject were about to be pronounced.

Members in general thanked God for Mr. K.'s long and dependable service in the church school and considered him a pillar of leadership. Even though he ran against the grain of some because they detected an undercurrent of arrogance, he was still generally considered good-natured and deeply religious.

At a meeting of the board of Christian education the chairman suggested the election of an assistant superintendent to take the place of Mr. K. if and when he should move to another position. The chairman had discussed this with him last week in private and he seemed to have no objections. Mr. K. kept aloof from the discussion of the board, and it was decided to take it up again at the next meeting. Evidently Mr. K. had numerous conferences with friends during the following month. No less than ten important members called the chairman to express shock that he saw fit to oust the present leader after so many devoted years.

When the meeting convened, the chairman was subjected to extremely critical remarks, so severe, in fact, that he was dumbfounded. Mr. K. offered to resign if that would "aid the cause of Christ." The board finished its work by adopting a vote of confidence in Mr. K. and accepting with regret the resignation of the chairman.

In the following months members got the hint that the chairman had attempted to intimidate the superintendent, and was responsible for the lack of progress in key areas of the church school. The insidious pressure on the former chairman mounted. He and his family left the church. Mr. K. expressed deep sorrow over this, and stated that the only reason he did not attempt to stop the departure was that the peace and well-being of the Body of Christ were above personal sentiment and the loyalty of friendship. The matter was far from concluded, however, for it appeared that the former chairman also had many friends in the church and the tension was aggravated. The pastor and the official board began to work sedulously to quiet the troubled waters.

❖ ❖ ❖

The question is often asked, "How is it that such seemingly dedicated Christians have no idea of the depth and intensity of their vindictiveness?" Partially the answer lies in the unconscious nature of explosive neurotic emotions. The neurotic cannot, *must* not, see himself as being filled with hostility. Partially these feelings emerge disguised. Vindictiveness to the disturbed personality is never aggression, but the Lord's justice working through him. Even in the throes of a flagrant negative set he may profess to allies a feeling of sympathy for his target. If the target is guilty of any sins, he capitalizes on them to the hilt. He can spot and magnify out of all proportion the hypocrisy in others of which he is guilty, and accusation against others is supposedly a means of absolving himself from similar transgressions.

What is the religious status and nature of the neurotic's Christian experience? In church, more often than not you will find him to be rather mystical, professing piety, holding at least one official position, noted for a monopoly of one special area (choir direction, work with youth, director of finances, president of women's work) which over the years he considers his private domain. He takes pride in a glowing religious conversion if this happened to him recently. If he has strong trends toward resignation and escapism, he is probably not on the board, and often sulks somewhere in the background as a martyr. Frequently we find overly compliant and self-effacing women (who have thoroughly driven any vindictiveness underground) hovering continually over the pastor, ready to do his bidding on a moment's notice. If there are accompanying trends of expansiveness and dictatorship, and if the pastor gives such a woman a free hand, future ministers find they must either reckon with her power or look for another church.

There is a strong ascendant-submissive relationship among neurotic personalities in church. Compliant ones are certain that a promising future hinges on dependence upon expansive-vindictive persons. This will be elaborated when we come to the expansive-vindictive person.

When the Creator confronts us with our sins, forgiveness helps us to know ourselves. The light of Christ touches the heart and the spectrum shades of emotion burst out into an arching rainbow of God's everlasting peace.

It takes sparks of courage and imagination inherent in manhood and womanhood to be saved. We must dare to believe that after lost years of idolatry and rebellion against the Creator, He still loves us and has always been willing to make *any sacrifice* to bring us home to our true beings—even the sacrificial suffering, death and resurrection of His own Son. As Søren Kierkegaard once declared, "The Christian heroism . . . is to venture wholly to be oneself, as an individual man, alone before the face of God."

The healthy individual in Christ may not know himself solidly, but he has no fear of self-discovery. If he is in the act of daring to be the man Christ envisions, he can be himself in the world, with any threats and risks that involves. He can dare to love for the sake of his soul's need to love, without first demanding that the world requite that love on his conditions. He can give himself to those who need love, despite the risk that God Himself took: the gamble that those who need love most may be the first to betray it. Lastly, he can learn to defend himself in a world often hostile, without scars closing off the ministering love of the Lord Jesus Christ through him.

The neurotic case is essentially different. In early years the emotionally disturbed individual is haunted by the lag between the idealized image and his actual personality. He may lean heavily on his power of reason to construct the whole of his environment to his imaginative patterns, or he may take refuge in the deepest kind of religious mysticism. A process of satellization upon Deity encourages him to lose himself in the arms of sovereign rule and order while sharing God's omnipotence. "By believing in a supreme deity the individual bolsters himself in the light of his own feelings of weakness, helplessness, and inferiority."

In numerous cases of a cataclysmic conversion of the neurotic personality we can trace guilt feelings due to the inability of the child to measure up to an angry parent's extremely industrious standards of superiority and prestige. God appears as a heavenly father who is angry because of transgressions of cosmic law. The doctrine of God's gracious acceptance through Christ's merits is received with intense relief and an earth-shaking reaction against worldly standards of success and glory.

The so-called normal personality is in varying degrees selective in reality. He chooses at different levels of consciousness the audiences before whom he displays his idols and with whom he feels at home. In coming to the true God he forsakes the idols and begins the upward process of adoring and learning to serve the Lord of Lords. God is seen through Christ, and the man is delighted with the discovery that sacrifice for this King is joy, and bondage to Him is freedom. His chief regret is that he acts so slowly on the discovery that surrendering to God an undivided loyalty increases the objects of his devotion and augments his power to love.

The neurotic personality is also relieved to forsake the wild cravings of idolatry. Gone forever are the lustings after gold, fortune, sexual conquest and worldly influence. What happens after that is a different story with every person. We have counseled neurotics who, through strident emotional upheavals, were making valiant attempts to gain self-knowledge and God-knowledge. In other cases we have been unsuccessful in efforts to lead the individual to a redemptive experience in Christ and the forsaking of idols, even though he combined neurotic ambition with endless hours of religious chores and church activities. Some had wonderfully transforming experiences—some in minutes, others over years—but they still brought hardship to the church because they irrevocably resisted the faintest revelation by the Spirit that they were attempting to re-create God in their images.

It seems that in all cases the neurotic also finds it difficult to resist periodic returns to his idol. Too often, by a wave of his mental scepter, he again converts all of reality to his audience. Too often when he enters the Kingdom he immediately senses the need for making God a trusted ally in idolatry. He is led by self-delusion into an artful identification with the righteous God, and we find this especially true when he has been brought up in a religious atmosphere.

"We should not attempt to formulate too easily any particular superiority striving; but we can find in all goals one common factor—a striving to be godlike. Sometimes we find children who express themselves quite openly in this way, and remark, 'I should like to be like God.' This idea of godlikeness appears in a more modest way in the idea of 'superman'; and it is revealing—I shall not say more—that Nietzsche when he became insane signed himself in a letter to Strindberg, 'The Crucified.'

". . . Once the goal of superiority has been made concrete, there are no mistakes made in the style of life. The habits and symptoms of the individual are precisely right for attaining his concrete goal; they are beyond all criticism."

By some bewildering paradox, the neurotic's pride in perfect humility, or in a glorious Pauline conversion, or in utter renunciation of sin, enables him to enter the sanctuary as a member of the privileged few. The words of the New Testament are given just the right subtle distortion to suit his personal framework. He is on mystically closer terms with God than the poor mass of Christians. He is a great believer in his prayer power. He is especially fond of those Biblical passages that identify the believer with Christ, and he often quotes Luther's remark that a Christian is "a little Christ." He glories in the fact that he has lost his life. As a human being he is no more. The merger with the Spirit is complete, and he takes seriously Christ's injunction to be perfect even as our Father in heaven is perfect. He is nothing at all; it is entirely God working and speaking through him. Compliments are passed off as rude misunderstandings. He could do nothing of himself; it is entirely of God.

He can do all things through Christ. He wields great power, for when he prays nothing will be denied him. He is above criticism. Things of the Spirit are spiritually discerned, and criticism only demonstrates the spiritual poverty of the critic. Since he is one of the Kingdom's inner circle, he always assumes all eyes are on him at any religious meeting. The people are surely waiting to hear what he will have to say. Now and then he will test their reactions by affirming a desire to remain in the background while others take the leadership for a change. But it is soon clear that any project of importance initiated without his approval or fulfilled without his blessing is regarded with contempt or bitter amusement. Anything not of "God" will fail.

In a number of these cases, the women are inveterate notewriters. It is only right and gracious that struggling souls should receive spiritual pearls from these women's treasures. Any member, particularly the sick and shut-ins, is likely to receive little spiritual notes in the most careful hand. These notes will be treasured, word will spread of the woman's goodness, and others will be dejected if she does not step forward with a word from God.

The more he can lose himself behind God, the safer the disturbed person feels. There is a conflict over whether to take the most prominent position and run the risk of failure or error, or to stay in the background as the power behind the throne. He prefers a little of both, although appearances before the public are anticipated with debilitating anxiety. It is discomfiting because he finds himself dependent on the approbation of the very people he regards as spiritual inferiors. It is better to be the great father who encourages the little ones to find their legs while he smiles benevolently from the wings. It is difficult to imagine the explosive content of the rage with which he regards presumptuous souls who fail to take his advice. But *he* is never displeased—it is God who is wrathful at those who hate Him. He feels, as the psalmist: "Do I not hate them that hate thee, O Lord?"

The neurotic identification with Deity in such a psychic pattern poses a bold challenge to depth therapy and pastoral theology. Some cases eventually demonstrate courageous ventures into health and wholeness through the tangled pathways of suffering, counseling, patient pastoral guidance, and through the mysterious and sovereign grace of God which relies upon life itself as the chief instrument of spiritual healing. Other cases stumble along for years, sensing the need for help and feeling bitterly disappointed with themselves for being weaklings. Still others become enraged at themselves for momentarily entertaining the insight that they have distorted the precious relationship of Christ to the believer into their imagined monopoly of Christ's power for the ends of a tyrannical idol. If they sometimes wonder why a volcano of rage always threatens to erupt below the veneer of calm perfection, the answer may be that spiritual souls encounter fierce struggles with Satan. If deep and abiding joy in salvation is missing, the answer they give themselves is that happiness is nothing; holiness is everything. They have built airtight cases for themselves.

The struggle to build an airtight case is an awesome labor to intensify human suffering. The counselor yearns to cry out, "Come back! Come to yourself and forsake an existence of pain without comfort, vision without insight, struggle without trust, and hope without peace. Come and give yourself to love again!"

But he does not come back, because if you said those words aloud he would not know what you were talking about. He does not see himself as a human being whose suffering does not have to be. In fact, only recently has science aided us to comprehend something of the depth of neurotic suffering. We have a long way to go in aiding a church with neurosis in her midst.

4
The Glory of the Power

IN THE DEVELOPMENT OF CIVILIZATION ONE OF THE ALMOST
insuperable barriers to peaceful co-operation is a sickness of
personality called expansive-vindictiveness. And yet, if we
were to poll ten persons at random, probably not one of the
ten would know what the term means.

All ten, however, would know much about the symptoms.
In international affairs the Hitlers play God in their wild
search for power and glory. Yes, in business some men are
more intent in viciously beating down their competitors than
in making a living. In families there are father-tyrants who
brook not a whisper of opposition. But do we place all these
in the same bundle? Is it a case of a relentless id? Is it rampant
egocentricity? Is it Adamic sin? Or is it a touch of racial madness in all of us?

Throughout the Bible arrogance is viewed as a protection
against the fears and uncertainties of life. There was vindictiveness in men such as Saul of Tarsus before their wills were
reconciled to the will of God through the cross of Christ.
But in our experience, in a drawer marked "Reserved for
Further Study," we have collected a mass of data that seems
to defy our easy religious categories. We see a group of calm,
efficient, intelligent, often charming persons—many of them
religious—who have made vindictiveness not merely a temporary response to hurts or cherished prejudices, but a veri-
table way of life. When once the psychic trigger is pulled they
are bent, in their suave but ruthless ways, on humiliating or
even destroying another human being.

What motivates such persons? Why and how do they find their ways into the hearts of our churches? What are they trying to accomplish? How can we help them?

As we have seen in the last chapter, the person who puts up an unconscious struggle against acute and chronic anxiety finds refuge by soaring above the battle. He finds safety through imagined glory. We have yet to discuss the three concrete images his idealized self may take in its attempt to patch together the conflicting areas of personality.

We said "concrete images," but this is not quite accurate. Three possibilities—three magnetic poles, if you will—always exert their forces, but the neurotic trends toward one for the sake of being a whole person. He may emphasize the image of an adored and adoring person (compliance), or a perfect and aloof person (detachment), or an omnipotent master of life (expansive-vindictiveness).

The first "type" attains ascendancy by "loving" everyone to death. The second gropes for safe, silent superiority. But the type we are concerned with here has turned to an outright attack. He is a flawless, superior being, a master of life. He is fortified against the vicissitudes of life, so what can hurt him? Now this is magic if it works. How does he hope to do it?

The expansive type can manage the advertising of his glory through *narcissism,* or *perfectionism,* or *aggressive vindictiveness.* In narcissism there is the strong element of pharisaism because this individual takes his eyes off the world and fastens them on the wonder of his idealized self. He is in love with the charm, the wonder, the power of himself and his gifts. A high I.Q. is there, and usually outstanding gifts, but he is not so much concerned with proving his capabilities as in assuming them.

After the youth meeting the pastor sat down with the young people. Placing a well-worn Bible before them, he said, "The Holy Spirit gives us all gifts. Mine is the gift of prophecy. Open any place at all in this Book and I can make a sermon from the text in ten minutes."

One girl took the book. "You mean, even if I open to some hard parts in, say . . . Exodus here . . . or Song of Solomon?"

"Of course," replied the minister. "In fact, sermons come easier from there than from some places in the New Testament." Everyone looked suitably impressed. The president of the group smiled. "You mean you get paid six thousand dollars for working five or ten minutes a week?" The group's laughter turned to a nervous titter when a scowl crossed the pastor's face. He changed course and replied, "If the sermon is good in five minutes, imagine how good it gets in a week!" Everyone smiled appropriately and seemed glad to change the subject.

◙ ◙ ◙

In this case the pastor did not expect to feel vindictive with mere boys and girls. His hostility only proved that "the president was becoming too bright for his own good."

In group conversation the disturbed personality maintains a guarded alert to detect signs of criticism or rejection of his position. Richard Wallen discusses speech styles in this connection: "Can this style of speaking control anxiety? Yes, if the person feels that certain kinds of intellectual achievements confer status or acceptance. . . . Narcissistic speakers insert feeling and preference reactions throughout their talk. Almost any topic offers them a chance to express their own appetites and aversions; and these feeling reactions are conveyed by means of superlatives and extreme figures of speech."

We might also mention the compulsion to talk. It seems

that the expansive-vindictive person is driven by a demon to get the spotlight and hold it. He cannot stop himself, and any hints that he is talking too much make an inferno of his rage.

If the layman began psychoanalyzing his friends, we would be in a sorry fix. You look at expansive-vindictiveness, and on the surface there is nothing to see but charm and a little too much pride. Why not? Everyone *knows* he is a person of extraordinary insight and razor-edge correctness. Don't they? Doesn't everyone simply assume that he's right? "There are people who either live so much in the imagination that in their own minds they are without blemish, or they have so covered themselves with a protective layer of militant rightness that everything they do, *eo ipso, is* right. Injuries to their pride can come only from the outside. Any questioning of their motivations, any uncovering of a handicap is felt as an insult. They can but suspect malicious intent in any person who does this to them."

A church pastor is God's prophet, ordained to proclaim the Word. Unfortunately, before he is able to detect neurotic trends in the narcissistic person he may give advice, offer a Bible verse, or make some criticisms without the utmost gentleness. The results are that in the middle of the conversation the church member turns purple with rage and becomes the minister's bitter enemy. "The simple fact that others have wishes or opinions of their own, that they may look at him critically or take exception to his shortcomings, that they expect something of him—all these are felt as a poisonous humiliation and arouse a smoldering resentment. He may then explode in a burst of rage and go to others who 'understand' him better."

In this regard the pastor is at a disadvantage. Without being aware of it he may have touched off an explosion and may not discover it until months later when he finds himself an open target in an all-out offensive.

The expansive person also advertises his glory through *perfectionism*. Here, too, we can detect the heavy influence of the psychic pole of detachment in the direction of pharisaism. There is no flight or pouting, supervening frustration, but more the determination to humiliate the enemy critic.

In perfectionism a grand program of performance is undertaken. The neurotic observes a rigid code of ethics and high standards in work. He loses his temper infrequently, partially because he seems completely indifferent to his own failures. He is unquestionably angry with himself for errors, but externalizes his self-hate and condemns others for their immorality.

▣ ▣ ▣

Mr. L. was a prominent member of the board of trustees. On occasion he would rebuke other members for errors of judgment. The pastor or another officer would find it necessary to make excuses for him.

One afternoon in the church office the pastor began to speak to him about certain traits that were antagonizing officers and endangering the spiritual progress of the church. Mr. L. cut him off and stormed out of the office. For the next eight years he remained an outspoken enemy of the minister. His charge was that the pastor had attacked him with rancor and demanded he resign from the board. Of course, the pastor made no such demand, but for eight years Mr. L.'s story never changed, and no doubt, in his own mind, he had come to be positive that he heard this, or that it was undoubtedly implied.

Interestingly enough, this person had a typical claim on life that his prestige and excellent performance in the Christian life entitled him to good health, good luck and long life.

After the eight years he became seriously ill and was taken to a hospital. He was so shaken by this "lack of faithfulness on God's part" that it appeared depression was causing him to lose his mind. The pastor visited him daily to minister the Word in love. Mr. L. experienced such helplessness that the very repressed psychic role of dependence came to the fore and he became quite dependent on the minister. Visitations continued for five weeks. Mr. L. was taken into eternal life, but several days before he died he confided to his wife a closeness to God he had never known before.

▣ ▣ ▣

While vindictiveness is the most prominent characteristic of this neurotic group, the third form of this expansiveness is *arrogant vindictiveness*. All other shades of neurosis have some feelings of love and loyalty that hold hostility in check, but the arrogant-vindictive person makes retaliatory triumph a style of life. Competition and conflict are his native air. Struggle to the bitter end, with victory at the last, is his dream. When he fastens his hostility on a target, he broadcasts to one and all that the target hates him, and for the good of everyone he must humiliate or destroy him. He cannot rest until he has proved his worth to himself and his power before others by slaying the dragon while whistles blow, flags fly and crowds cheer. And should the poor unfortunate dragon defend himself, the vindictive considers this some form of cheating. It is the final outrage! In fact, everyone knows the dragon-slayer is a man of peace and good will. By defending himself, the dragon is simply disturbing the peace and needlessly prolonging the conflict.

This neurotic also assures himself of his rightness by testing his power. It should be merely enough for him to raise a finger and all obstacles will disappear. One word from him and the minister must pack and leave. He says calmly, "Don't worry

about a thing. I can handle this little difficulty in no time."
If the pastor does not take the first train out, he feels that God
has been insulted and he must avenge His honor.

When a target is in plain view, there is good reason to
let out all the vindictiveness that has been piling up for so
many years and from so many sources. Month after month,
year after year, the target's mistakes—real or imagined—are
recorded in his mind or in a notebook.

▣ ▣ ▣

The church of a small southern city found itself in the
suburbs and growing fast. A most compliant, self-effacing
minister had pampered about ten prominent families who
had been with the church for at least fifteen years. His successor was aggressive, younger, and intent on winning many
persons for Christ and building a deeply spiritual congregation to contradict the stereotype of a fat and too-contented
suburban church.

The leading couple of the church had worked hard for lo,
these many years. They obviously resented the training of
newcomers and their nomination to official positions, Mr.
and Mrs. A. could see their influence and prestige waning and
told the new minister that he was plainly making a mistake in
encouraging Pentecostalists on the one hand (and by that
they meant anyone with less education and a more religious
attitude than they possessed), and nonspiritual persons on the
other (meaning anyone with more education and the same
degree of commitment), to take leadership in the church.
The pastor suggested that the couple talk things over in the
office. They came but their conversation was irrelevant to the
problem, although they were courteous.

Mr. and Mrs. A. were the counseling couple for the senior
high youth group. The minister was disturbed when the
young people said he was being openly criticized by Mrs. A.

He was dumbfounded when, at the next meeting of the board of stewards, Mr. A. undertook to explain for an hour a long written list of incidents in which the minister had failed in his work, had hurt others, and had even acted immorally.

When a representative of the denomination came to speak to the pastor and Mr. and Mrs. A., the list was so long and impressive that he privately indicated to the minister, "Where there's smoke, there's fire."

One of the charges was that the minister had a ministerial student assisting him in the services of worship. The bishop replied to a letter from the pastor by sanctioning this practice, agreeing that if it were done no more than once a month it would encourage other students and would be good experience for this one. When this letter was read at the next meeting of the board, that criticism was quickly dropped, but by then Mr. A. had several others—all devastating.

The pastoral relations committee and the quarterly conference agreed that the peace of the church was being disturbed and the pastor would do better in a different parish. He resigned and was transferred to a church in another state.

▣ ▣ ▣

There are several reasons why the denominational representative gave the advice he did, and we shall discuss them later. He knew nothing of the dynamics of the problem and had neither the time nor the inclination to search them out, even if he had had the psychological background to enable an interpretation in depth. He concluded that the problem wasn't clearing up, Mr. and Mrs. A. were such faithful workers in the church that they apparently had had no trouble with the previous minister, and the list was so long—so the case against the minister must have enough truth in it to warrant his leaving.

In this case Mr. and Mrs. A. (and Mrs. A.'s sister, two of her friends and Mr. A.'s brother) felt that their continuous, hostile attack on the pastor was entirely justified by the list of his shortcomings. If they had been forced to give any reason why God chose them to be the instruments of His holy justice, it would no doubt have been the rationalization that Mr. A. was officially commissioned to guard the peace and unity of the church, and that their official position, superior spiritual enlightenment and long record of service entitled them to this task. What they would have failed to understand was that these same qualities supposedly *entitled* them to control both the pastor and official board, and once frustrated, their *claims* for control rested on the broader base of having been allegedly attacked. They announced to everyone that they felt sorry for the pastor, but knew that he was hostile toward them.

At this point Karen Horney makes an important observation: "More specifically, his [the vindictive person] claims are demands for retribution for injury done. In order to solidify this basis for claims he must, as it were, treasure and keep alive injuries received, whether ancient or recent. He may compare himself to the elephant who never forgets. What he does not realize is his vital interest in not forgetting slights, since in his imagination they are the bill to present to the world. Both the need to justify his claims and his responses to their frustration work like vicious circles, supplying a constant fuel to his vindictiveness."

It is of prime importance to comprehend the dynamics of this vindictiveness. First note its *intensity*. On an imaginary line drawn between the poles of detachment and expansive-vindictiveness, any point closer toward the vindictive side would remind us of the character appearing in many pages of the Bible but typified especially by Absalom, David's son (see II Samuel). There is the slow, careful building of a following by a capable person urbanely bent on self-aggrandizement. He lusts for a place adequate to the significance of his idol and one that supports it. That place may be on the throne or discreetly behind it. But the swift and merciless attack on his unsuspecting prey leaves no public doubt as to who considers himself the boss.

In case after case we find the denomination sends a busy minister, or possibly a retired layman previously active in industrial personnel relations, to sit in with the factions. Other disputes and difficulties in church life have been dealt with by God's grace through pastor and consecrated laymen. The intervention of a third party is evidence that the minister is blocked by an insuperable obstacle. And yet, after some advice, "Let's you and he patch things up like nice fellows," falls on deaf ears, and after some hasty tricks in group dynamics fail, the conciliatory party is usually willing to grant, after one or two hours, that the advice of the angry layman is best and the minister ought to leave. No doubt the demand for the pastor to leave seems rather harsh, to say the least, but this occurs so often that there doesn't seem much anyone can do. Few are willing or able to study the harshness and its relevance to the total problem.

The expansive person is not able to reach compromise. If he were, no intervention would have been necessary. He meets with the conciliatory party to make others understand the intensity of the mental cruelty he bears. This "cruelty" is the basis for his demands, and as long as the pastor remains, he *is* miserable, and *does* feel threatened, and is positive the church cannot thrive unless he is happy. Any suggestion of agreement or forgiveness or charity strikes him as insulting. It appears to him as a suggestion that he obstruct justice and be untrue to himself in order to present his opponent with victory on a silver platter. What he is saying, in effect, is, "As long as I am suffering, the Kingdom of God must remain at a standstill." This type rules by what looks suspiciously like blackmail.

The second characteristic of vindictiveness is its *duration*. Everyone in the church may tread lightly, but day after day, month after month, the hostility gets worse. Time itself does not heal vindictiveness. Once the die is cast, this person's privileged status is placed on the line. Thereafter the very presence of the minister is a personal affront. The growth and prosperity of the congregation appear to him as temporary victories for the opponent, and he will go so far as to advise new prospects not to join the church "just yet." When responsible members of the congregation are about to conclude that he is pacified, he opens a new phase of opposition.

He is, remember, somewhat afraid of retaliation. He is fond of hiding (as are many "normal" persons, of course) behind the word "they." He makes some of his vindictiveness contagious by collecting chance remarks, blowing them up out of all proportion to their context, and brandishing the word "they." "They say . . ." this, and it is very serious. "They say . . ." that, and maybe one person said it, or none, but it is "they." And, of course, quite a few persons may have a legitimate criticism of the pastor, and if so, many persons constitute the imposing demon called "they."

"They" usually means one or more persons in the church's powerful ruling corps, called the "power structure." This structure may contain elements of competition, suspicion or antagonism, but it rarely gets out of hand or comes to the attention of the denomination. The following reasons tell us why.

First, the families that make up the power structure are often related by blood or marriage. Second, if the outstanding layman has these expansive trends, he is yielded to by the others who have neurotic trends because: a) he has greater prestige in terms of money, business position, spiritual gifts, natural talents (such as teaching the adult class or speech-making); b) he serves the denomination and its officials with continuing responsibility and without pay; c) he has an important responsibility on the official board; d) he has worked sedulously for the church over the years; e) he has built up a following of close friends in key positions on the church boards, on all-church nominations committees, and in pastoral relations committees.

Third, these persons have no intention of declaring war on each other when they depend on the church for admiration, respect and obedience. Ministers come and go, but the people at home must be lived with indefinitely.

Fourth, each has carved out a sphere of influence. One may be the director of youth choirs and children's work, another may be a key person in men's work, another may be the force-to-be-reckoned-with in the women's society. Expansive and pharisaic persons may secretly delight in knowing each other's sins, but they have a need for each other. If they cannot control the rest of the church directly, they can bargain with the persons who control each part.

Fifth, all unite in employing the minister as the instrument of peace and the co-ordinator of spheres of influence. The minister knows that if he fails to do this, they will immediately unite to expel him.

The reasonably normal Christian soon develops affection for his pastor. He has not the slightest desire to control anything or anyone, and when the pastor is attacked he is deeply shocked. If he is personally involved in a church dispute he seeks the help of Christ through his minister, and if he further disturbs the church he will usually retire from active church life until Christ is able to minister His grace to all. Or, if he must, the normal Christian will worship at another church. If his personality clashes with that of the pastor, he will work it out with him in prayer and conference, or, if the worst occurs, he will leave the church rather than disturb its spiritual impact on the community. If the minister seems to have deeply disturbing trends, the layman may not find he can discuss them with his pastor, in which case he feels the need to pray for him and discuss his feelings with an older, more mature and deeply spiritual member of the official board. The expansive neurotic, however, does not see the minister in this light. In his mind the minister should perform a definite function in protecting his sphere of influence and prestige in the church—which he regards as his personal club.

Nothing serious will occur outwardly if the pastor has deep trends of compliance and a need to be adored. He soon sees the handwriting on the wall and bows to the mutual-security arrangement in defense of his own security. In this case the expansive individual may disparage him as a quiet, mousy, ineffectual person, and may declare that because the pastor lacks sense and administrative ability the key laymen must do most of the work. The truth is that he not only tolerates him, but also needs him. It is quite doubtful that trouble will ever seriously break out between such a minister and parishioner, although sparks will often fly between key persons. The expansive person may not respect the morbidly dependent pastor, but he knows he can afford to be cheerful, suave and even patronizing in church because he has little to fear.

When the pastor has aggressive trends, the situation is extremely difficult from the beginning. Expansive persons see the minister as a terrible threat to the whole church, and when we say they see this *right away,* we mean within two or three months after the minister arrives. They sense that *they* know the pastor like a book, and conclude that his spiritual sermons, visitations and acts of ministry are means of discomfiting them and strengthening his own position. The ensuing struggle is not a pleasant one. Compliant trends in the pastor may come to the fore, but his attempts at appeasement are regarded as ineffectual devices.

The questions we must ask are: How did these persons get that way? What are they doing in a Christian church in the first place? How can we help them?

In these cases the story of childhood is one of subjugation and humiliation. Tyrannical, rejecting and extremely opinionated parents belittled the attempts of the growing child to trust himself and learn who he was. He made suggestions that were laughed at; his opinions were unwanted or contradicted. He may have been outwardly friendly only because he had to be, but that was a safety facade. True feelings of warmth and rapport had to be crushed, and it was better to be sagacious and continually on guard. His true self had no place in a warring, crushing, hypocritical world.

The tragedy of this, simply put, is that a false conclusion about himself and humanity became ingrained in his very being. Even if he was brought up in an intensely religious home, he feels that people are out there and he is over here, and safety means being obeyed and respected as were his father and mother.

The neurotic's love of power and his paradoxical need for self-surrender of some kind is a conflict that has been reflected in philosophy and theology since the birth of man. To Nietzsche, son of generations of Lutheran pastors, nothing could be more despicable than weakness. The doctrine that the meek shall inherit the earth was enough to turn the stomach. The goal was power and freedom from the "Bible-dictated ethics of a decadent society." To Nietzsche, the herd existed solely to glorify the strong.

When the power-mad smell the rising fires of insanity in their conclusions, they seek some terms of accommodation with millions of neighbors and billions of stars. Nietzsche would have made more of self-discipline if it hadn't reeked so of Christianity. Now and then he let himself show kindness to the poor. Insanity was his only sure destination.

The expansive-vindictive person, however, does not make an open grab for glory unless he has actual traces of psychosis. Don't forget that his symptoms originally grew out of a fear of power, of parents, of his own weakness, of his anxiety, and a fear of the suspicions and hostility of others. There are safer, more devious means of arrogating glory to one's self.

The philosophers did not openly grab for glory. They looked for a kind of submission. Schopenhauer submitted to a form of nirvana and renounced striving and the lusts of the will. The ascetics turned their backs on the glory and pomp of fading time. We shall note in another chapter that the detached person renounces the world and submits to the masses as a patronizing god of perfection. The compliant type submits to "love and service." To what does the expansive person submit?

The question interests us because with the Scripture's stress on humility, kindness, forebearance, and servanthood, you might suppose that church would be the last place he would be found. Neurotics outside the church are repulsed by their association of Christ with helplessness, meekness, forgiveness, and submission to His enemies. When the expansive person *is* in the church it is usually because strict parents made him attend as soon as he could.

When he finds himself in church it is rare that he takes a back seat. Religion is very important to him. And he *does* experience deep religious feelings, a kind of relief at "giving up" the lust after power and glory which smells of insanity. He has learned only too well that the Hitlers call for the world's armies to strike them down.

He submits *first* of all to God's power. To the detached person, the evident fact about God is His holiness, while to the compliant one it is His love. To the expansive type, it is His power. The God of power gives His power to those who serve Him well. This does not mean that the expansive neurotic has no use for God's love. On the contrary, he often reminds people about God's love, and especially when someone becomes self-assertive or antagonizes him.

Second, the expansive character submits also to the role of Messiah, which is different from the role of bondservant or the detached but patronizing comrade. His almost total preoccupation is with the fulfillment of his talents and his role or leadership. He will run the building campaign just right, and the ushering, and the serving of communion, and the board of trustees. No one in the church can do it as well as he can, and the congregation ought to be grateful for his expert hand. He is always uneasy about the power and authority of the minister, and knows right well that if, by a turn of fate, he were the minister, matters would be taken care of like magic.

Third, he is submissive to the Christian ethic in the sense that he endorses it. He endorses it by his surface behavior and by using mistakes of others as a sword over their heads. In fact, the only two areas wherein this person can feel reasonably safe are at the head of a totalitarian society and in church. When he endorses the teaching of Christian love, he means that as the leader he must take certain liberties, of course, but others must always love him. He can hurt them but they must forgive, as Christ taught. He can give orders because the Bible says, "Yea, all of you be subject one to another, and be clothed with humility: for God resisteth the proud, and giveth grace to the humble." He can appear before the congregation as speaker and leader (a situation he dearly loves) without incurring envy, because envy is unchristian. It is obvious, or he knows it should be obvious to everyone, that he cannot be held accountable to the letter of the law as the other people must be. Most of the time they do not know what is best, until he tells them.

It is unfortunately true that some of his feelings of religious elation derive from successful undertakings in which due gratitude is expressed by the church. But he is never really happy. He fears envy and someone is always around to take exception or make a suggestion contrary to his. He wonders at his patience with people.

When we think of the ministry we realize how much work needs to be done in seminaries in psychological testing and counseling. It is a shame to send into the churches pastors in whom these expansive trends are deeply persistent. Much needs to be discovered concerning the significance of neurotic symptoms in religious guise.

The question for the church is, How can the expansive-vindictive personality be checked, the pastor protected, and the church's safety from his hostility maintained while competent persons attempt to lead him into a fruitful embrace of God in the depths of his true being? While he may profess a belief in the cross, how can he stand compassionately with his brothers in the sufferings that bring them to the suffering of the Son of man? What steps can he take toward becoming a whole person in order to bring wholeness to others who need self-esteem?

Let's admit that few of us have the training to counsel such a person over long periods of time. He will not go to the pastor regularly for help. And if he does go, under the pretext of discussing stewardship or theology, he will stop if he thinks for a moment that in some way *he* is expected to change. It takes an expert psychiatrist with many years of experience to provide therapy for the expansive person, and even then the results after three or four years may be bitterly disappointing. As we said in the beginning of this chapter, it is a tragic sickness of spirit. Everyone has seen the symptoms, some recognize the sickness; few can cure the illness.

Most of the pastors who have written or spoken to me wish these persons were out of their churches. These are honest feelings, but in a sense we wonder if God doesn't sometimes feel about most of us what we all usually feel about some of us. God committed Himself to saving all of us, and some of us crucified His Son. There was a time when we were despondent and disillusioned, and we turned at last to the Lord. If the disturbed person turns to the church he deserves to know God as He is, that he may find himself as he is.

We are troubled by the fact that he already has a religion of sorts. As Karen Horney remarks: "Nevertheless he lives in any case by his private religion (his idealized image), abides by his own laws (his shoulds), within the barbed-wire fence of his own pride and with his own guards to protect him against dangers from within and without. As a result he not only becomes more isolated emotionally but it also becomes more difficult for him to see other people as individuals in their own right, different from himself. They are subordinated to his prime concern: himself."

If this is so, it is not easy for us to affirm glibly that A is saved, and B is unsaved. God alone knows the human heart. Christ hath brought redemption, and now we must labor to bring it to men. There are men who labor and are crushed, and by many a tortuous path they finally find the Christ who is seeking them—and in a manner far different from Saul of

·79·

Tarsus. You cannot chart the Spirit's course; He works differently with every man. But in all cases He needs humble co-laborers with something of the patience of God Himself.

In dealing with this type of person, the pastor's greatest task is with himself. How imperative that precious hours be spent in prayer for those who need Him in ways they know not of! Nothing will be successful in therapy unless the Spirit of God roots out retaliation and impatience from the pastor's heart. After all, why is *he* so anxious? What is *he* trying to prove? How much does love motivate *him*? Whatever happens to the pastor and his family in a church, he must resolve to be honest with God, sincere with his soul, and true to his calling. It would be possible for him to win a battle in church and lose the struggle of his own spirit. If a Christian maintains his integrity, he is automatically a victorious person, and his years of usefulness stretch out to eternity.

As the leading officers and the pastor pray and read, various possibilities will present themselves. If the vindictive person has recently joined the church, the chances of helping him are excellent. Capable deacons can sponsor his integration into church life, tactfully pointing out when he is becoming dictatorial, and encouraging him to feel that he is an equal among equals. In office conferences the pastor can discover ways of demonstrating acceptance. Deep within himself the disturbed person hopes that the spiritual leader will love him and work with him.

Experience will tell the pastor how and when to "structure" his conferences and telephone calls so that the vindictive person does not make monopolizing demands on his time and spirit. He should be given tasks that mobilize his talents and still allow him to feel that the limits inherent in a co-operating church do not imply rejection of him. He certainly should not be placed on any official board if the pastor entertains doubts about the wisdom of it. If the pastor has a mature personality and is trusted, and if he has had some training in the field, the nominations committee should by all means listen to him when he says, "Brethren, I do not feel that Mr. A.'s main contribution to the Kingdom is through the official boards just yet. Perhaps later."

If the pastor walks into a church in which this person has been playing god for twenty years, then he has quite a task before him—and to think that this is exactly what happens to many young men just out of seminary! He can remember right away that he is the pastor to the whole flock. He can also remember this truth: Through the Word, through the sacraments, through group discussion, through prayer, Christ does speak to and love this vindictive person. Sometimes the most we can hope for is to bring out into consciousness the tension between God's love and some of the symptoms of religious idolatry. The expansive member may never say to himself, "My life is built around the lust for superiority and prestige," but more and more his defenses can recede as he sincerely seeks God's will. I have witnessed the expansive-vindictive person moved to tears by a profound experience of Christ. Relief becomes a kind of joy. The fact that the pastor is not a superman and that this person may regress—rejecting submissiveness as helplessness—should not diminish our patience or our prayers.

Caution does not mean that the pastor should pull in the reigns of his program or curtail his message. If he preaches that God blesses healthy ambition and the desire to amount to something in life, it is too bad if the neurotic misinterprets the message. After all, not everyone who has feelings of inferiority is a neurotic person by a long shot.

The pastor may preach on idolatry and the lust for superiority and prestige, or the need for forgiveness and yieldedness before others, and someone may take offense—"The minister is picking on me from the pulpit." Well, *is* the minister picking on him? If not, then the Word of God must be given with courage. If the proclaimer of the Word cannot be true to his calling, he ought to leave the pastorate.

Later we shall discuss discipline and administration related to the oft-held conclusion that a man's ministry in a local church ought to end because there are some people he cannot help. Salvation is glorious because it is the end of a process that began with the tragedy of Christ's crucifixion by persons He could not heal.

A final word about the expansive-vindictive person who, in a profound conversion experience, gives himself whole-heartedly to the labors of Christ and increasingly demonstrates trends of compliance. He will want to follow the pastor around continually in dependence on his prestige and leadership. What a temptation to give such a person every loose rope and open berth in the church! He would take every opportunity to do everything—and he would end up antagonizing everyone, and feeling rejected himself. He would be quite a thorn to the next minister.

If persons in this group begin on the right track, however, they can be a great asset to the Lord. We have found men's discussion groups genuinely useful. No man is permitted to monopolize their discussions and each is given a task without luxuriating in the spotlight. The fellowship of the Spirit makes for deep respect for others and for the whole church. Certain laymen take newcomers under their wings and curtail the feeling that the whole Kingdom depends upon a favored few who were granted a Pauline conversion.

As I look back upon this group with compliant trends in conflict with their vindictiveness, I can see all now have responsible positions in the church and all have served their

Lord well. They still have a tendency to want the church to feel that if it weren't for them nothing vital would be done. "Only a few of us do the work, Pastor, and we're getting so tired. Oh, well." Considering what they have accomplished in the Lord's strength, the tolerance of their obnoxious traits has been a small price to pay. Even when their neurotic trends have been frustrated they sense that there is the difference of heaven and hell between what happened to them in the church and what was happening to them in the world.

5

The Fears
of the Parasite

THE LOSING OF ONE'S LIFE IN ORDER TO SAVE IT IS A PARADOX
that escapes the sinful and is distorted by the neurotic. The
problem of its seeming contradiction is clearly witnessed in
its extremes in the case of an alcoholic both sinful and neurotic. In undergoing treatment he infers that he has been too
preoccupied with self. He must forget himself. He must lose
himself by being devoted to something or someone else. Very
well. He then trends to an obsequious attachment to em-
ployer, talented person or relative. When he is shunned or
abused he returns to bitterness and berates himself for having
been so dependent. Now he resolves to stand on his own two
feet. His arrogance further alienates him, and he continues
where he left off with his drinking. Now what shall he do?

The striving for self-confidence ended in arrogance. You
cannot tell him to be humble because he already resents being
a doormat. How can he lose himself when he is already lost?
How can he be self-assertive and aggressive without becoming
a little tin god? How can he gain possession of himself and
surrender himself at one and the same time? How can he surrender his self without becoming fawning and servile? How
can he be poised and self-reliant without turning toward
arrogance and detachment?

While Gardner Murphy sees the paradox as beyond adjust-
ment, Wayne Oates agrees that it is irreconcilable on logical
grounds, and avers that the incarnation and crucifixion of

Christ bring new selfhood into focus so that "The contradiction of self-surrender and self-realization is overcome in personal participation in the Gospel."

There can be no question that the gospel does call for total self-surrender. The human being was created to expend himself through a wealth of spiritual, physical and mental resources. He gives of himself when he enhances the intrinsic qualities of something or someone else, and brings to fruition in another entity that which is worthy, true, good, and beautiful. The more one is captured by this "other," whether it be the directing of a symphony or the loving of a woman, the more one must expend himself. He thus grows in satisfaction, strength, fulfillment and purpose. Love will demand us; but all love will disappoint us save the eternal love of Him who created and knows us. The rash gravitation toward sex in times of spiritual decay is a symptom of the need to find security through dependence in a manner that provides the maximum sensual pleasure. The selfish and impossible demand that the sexual partner become a god to provide both pleasure and security, apart from growth and sacrifice on the other's part, is a guarantee of the despair that always supervenes the erection of gods in the place of God. Only the everlasting arms are able to hold us up while the eternal Spirit within us provides the invigorating hope for acceptance and maturity. In the enterprises of the Kingdom of Christ's love, this hope does not disappoint us.

There are many unconverted persons who use God and religion, and they are not necessarily neurotic—granting, of course, that psychiatry is not always agreed as to what constitutes neurotic trends. Outside of Christ, a so-called normal personality may honestly and confidently commit himself to worthy causes and persons, or he may idolize some person or movement as a projection of his own rampant egotism. His restlessness is due to an inability to discover that which he can identify himself with in honesty and confidence. Partly this is due to certain insecurities within himself and the possible instability or dishonesty of the "other." Two pitfalls he cannot avoid are sham and boredom. He must always measure up to the requirements and expectations of other projects and persons so as to avoid rejection. Select and safe routines are settled upon in order to avoid humiliation. The unsaved person cannot understand why the search for self-confidence is a dark detour, and the goals of security and acceptance drain life of zest. Certainly the sporadic binges in search of zest mark a hapless reaction against goals unworthy of the total human being.

The persons in whom we should trust in providing acceptance and encouraging self-surrender—while creating the environment in which confidence grows through forgiveness —are our parents. The striving for growth, or we should say, the struggles in the growing processes, comprise trends of satellization (dependence while appropriating their strength), de-satellization and re-satellization.

In our society, men in general fare badly in making the transition from dependence to self-surrender, and from de-satellization to fulfillment. They are wary of dependence except when self-surrender is desirable in a manly (sexual) role. Men love the company of other men for there they luxuriate in their collective protestations of independence. Women, on the other hand, tend to accept their role of dependence, and disguise it as mothering and dominating when it has been denied them and they are suspicious of their ability to merit sexual love.

In many congregations the women vastly outnumber the men. Partly we have a watered-down gospel to blame for this. Jesus meek and mild is held up as our example, and salvation (if that word is even used) is allegedly found by following in His steps. Men are repulsed on two grounds: 1) Why and how can a man grow strong by turning over his independence to another male? and, 2) Why turn it over to one so effeminate? It is not without good reason that the Virgin Mary has gained such a prominent role in enabling a feeling of religious dependence for so many wary persons.

The psychical tensions of personality ultimately converge in the searching of the self to identify itself in a tri-polar dimension of dependence, control over others, and detachment. The ego vacillates from one pole to another. Shall we lean on certain strong persons who we believe will give us love and protection, since our attempts at de-satellization were always highly unsatisfactory? Or, shall we become Apollos and overpower others with superior strength and prestige? Or, shall we play it safe and run from those who can hurt us?

When the so-called normal self accepts himself, it is not without anxiety that he hears he is lost unless he denies himself. The best of human love leads us astray unless it is hallowed by the love of God. Our best efforts betray us unless redeemed by the omniscient God. Where shall we turn in a world where we are damned if we do and damned if we don't? On this the Bible could not be clearer. Only the encounter with Jesus—powerful Carpenter and Friend of little children, Lion of Judah and Man of sorrows, whip-swinging Judge and gentlest Companion, terrible Judge and understanding Advocate, Leader of men and Servant of God, crucified in love and raised in glory—can demand life and give it, can hallow the gamble of love with eternal forgiveness, and can challenge us to spend ourselves while healing our wounds.

If the task of facing himself is difficult for the fairly stable man outside of Christ, it is more so for the neurotic. He continually vacillates in the tri-polar dimension. But early in life, in answer to the question, "Who am I, really?" the neurotic trends toward one of the poles. Beneath the surface the three poles continually send out magnetic calls for self-expression. In gravitating toward one pole, the individual unconsciously attempts a solution for his conflicting trends. In some persons it seems that two magnetic pulls are equally at work, their emphases depending on the person's roles at work, home, club and church. The club would find him giving more liberal expression to expansive solutions (dominance over others), while at church he is the loving and dependent saint. Then again, critical situations may cause an about-face. One solution of retreat and independence seemed to be eliminated when the patient moved to another city and became morbidly dependent upon an arrogant-vindictive person. More commonly the neurotic individual will turn toward one of the three poles, and his experiences of school, adolescence and religious conversion or rebellion will tend to cement the cast in one direction or another.

In an analysis of personality dynamics, it is necessary to perceive the workings of the self-effacing solution, or neurotic dependency. Often the most religious persons in the church are in this group. This solution is perplexing because it usually results in intense sacrifice for God and His church, while it causes suffering to the disturbed person. It often brings hardship to pastor and local church.

For this individual there is no question of salvation through self-surrender. He is certain that he *has* surrendered himself completely. He has committed himself. Love has captured him and arrogance has disappeared. He has lost himself and is being expended. It is not always clear what he is supposed to surrender to, but he knows himself as a self-surrendering soul.

His traumatic experiences with a "glorious" person in his

family, or with a despotic but benevolent father, or a Queen Bee, guilt-causing mother who spoiled him at the price of unquestioned obedience, led him to raise the white flag of truce early. He soon sued for peace and threw himself on the mercy of the court.

His motto is *"Victory through unconditional surrender!"* The net effect is that he has already used his own version of the gospel to forge a counterfeit salvation. If he has made a profession of faith, he has come upon the dynamics of a Spirit-filled community as a useful expression of his neurotic solution. This solution is the obtaining of power through self-abnegation. He says to the fellowship, in effect, "What do you preach? Self-surrender? I have surrendered myself without stint. Love for others? My whole life is devoted to love. Being accepted? I am dependent upon God for acceptance, without reservation. Vicarious suffering? How often I have felt the pain of another and suffered for him! The cross symbolizes my life. Service for others? My one thought is a completely unselfish life, holily and trustingly dedicated to the good of others." This indeed seems to be his life, and if he has unconscious motives and conflicting designs he can honestly say he is rarely aware of them.

This neurotic solution is one of the many "deals" that persons unconsciously make with life. Here is a person who feels inferior in a vast land of growling gods. The safest course of action is to throw in the towel and become a devoted ally, take the center of gravity out of the self and place it in others —and sooner or later in one. This course is envisioned as a Garden of Paradise." "Few people," he declares, "are really bad. They will all be touched if I am jolly and adorable. Any outwardness and excessive ambition in myself must be sacrificed in case I encounter someone who needs to be appeased."

Hostility in himself must be shaken off as a duck throws off water. In any dispute he must admit he is wrong and ask for forgiveness. There is no use in arguing. If you argue, sooner or later someone will get offended. If you feel cheated, there is no point in being boorish and making an issue of it. Forget it. Let it ride.

In every situation he encounters, this type of person follows certain strict rules. One is to jump at the chance to do favors for people. Their slightest wish is his command. Another is to inflate others and let them know how much you think of them. Another rule is to belittle yourself and your efforts in a joking manner so that others will be tempted to contradict you and say how good you are. These rules are never to be broken.

This person has a horror of ridicule. He demeans himself enough as it is, and public humiliation is more than he can take. But if embarrassment does come, it is better to take it lying down than to fight back. Timidity is despised, but, on the other hand, if you give in to people and tell them how wonderful they are, sooner or later they will like you and will refrain from ridiculing or rejecting you.

The question arises, What does this person worship as an idol? The answer is that he worships a picture of himself as a person kind, magnanimous, humble, gracious, affable, and a great one to give and take a joke. The very salt of the earth! He has no use for the expansive-vindictive pole, and has a dread of losing his temper. His true self is so diminished and beaten that he unconsciously yearns to lash out at all the beasts who have taken advantage of his good nature and have made a fool of him. But he dares not. No, that must *never* happen! If he antagonizes others, what might they not do to him? He may feel guilty, but self-hate must not be external- ized. Unfortunately, he cannot altogether escape the feeling that not only does he hate himself, but many persons hate him. He must not, however, admit this. Better to forget self and think of others as kind and generous. In time they will accept his goodness and respond in mutuality. (The ingrates!)

The "hook" in his service is quite pointed indeed. The claims of the all-sacrificing father or mother are clear enough. A mental note is made of years of selflessness in behalf of the children. No labor for them was ever too great. And now that the years have swiftly passed, the children learn of all that one or both parents have done. If, for example, father's demands are not met and love fully returned (as he interprets love), he will not scold. But the grown children can expect to feel guilty. It will be apparent to everyone that they have matched parental sacrifice with ungratefulness, if not moral insensibility. Rather than live with this guilt, the children will decide to "do everything to make father's days happy." Occasionally, one or two of the children may decide that a complete severance of relations is preferable to beatings with the rod of guilt.

Markedly characteristic of the self-effacing solution is the fear of loneliness. When the true self is thoroughly beaten, and the personality is weakened by the conflict between latent vindictiveness and the need to demonstrate love and generosity, the morbidly dependent neurotic must attach himself as a parasite to another. It is as if he crowns a seemingly superior person in order to say, "Now love me. Lift me up, carry me about. Let me bask in your power and generosity. Let me be your glowing satellite. Take the responsibility for my safety." He is willing to suffer insult and injury if this "host" will continue to accept him as bosom companion.

If this type of neurotic is an unmarried male, he feels challenged by an independent woman who is untouched by his compliments. If she strikes him as cool, calm and confident, but continues to show a flirtacious interest at arm's length, he will likely develop some kind of serious "crush" on her.

One can imagine the place of sexual love in this constellation! It takes on the coloring of a base groveling of slave before master. The object of adoration becomes all in all. Nothing is worth while unless she shares it with him. Neither art nor poetry can describe the parasite's elation when his beloved responds with interest or even affection. Unfortunately, a weird cycle makes for continued deterioration of personality. The dependent person is likely to mistake arrogance for self-confidence, independence for strength. He enjoys seeing in the other what is repressed in himself. He assumes the other must be a Rock of Gibraltar when in reality this partner is often an irresponsible weak reed unable to enter into a healthy spirit of rapport and mutual obligation. Consequently, the self-effacing individual is often rejected and hurt by her, and in response to his fear of loneliness he throws himself that much harder on her mercy. He will do anything, *anything,* if she will let bygones be bygones and love him!

Incident in a China Shop

He felt uneasy, but reasons he could not find
And did not wish to, as long as she remained kind
And gracious, gentle and soothing, charming and quick of
    mind.

Of her gentility he was too much aware;
Felt, in her presence, clumsy; in himself, a fear
That, stepping back, he'd break something he hadn't known
    was there.

And so he broke her heart.
Much as a curious browser who picks up an antique teacup
Admiringly, amused by its elegance, intrigued by its
    quaintness,

Might, upon returning it to the shelf, having decided it was
    not for him,
Drop it, accidentally, and watch, with only the most fleeting
    regret,
How easily and thoroughly it shattered,
He broke her heart.

She helped sweep up the pieces, insisted it was not his fault,
    not peeved.
(He had not thought it was. She credited him with feelings
    finer than any he conceived.)
She said politely it was a trivial matter. He, naturally,
    believed.

Strangely enough, when the parasite is accepted to any safe
degree he opens a psychic steam valve to permit a thin jet
stream of self-abuse to come into conscious recognition. At
this point, any expansive drives he has been harboring come
to the fore and he tries to control the beloved and vent some
of the pent-up vindictiveness. He may even become boastful
and dictatorial. If the relationship is broken he becomes
obsequious again and begs for mercy. We have counseled engaged and married couples who are alternately separated and
reconciled time after time. The independent or arrogant
partner gradually comes to feel that the self-effacing individual is a yoke around her neck, while he complains that he
cannot live with her or without her.

The self-effacing individual feels abused to begin with, but
when he will not permit recognition of an attack upon him
by friend or enemy he turns his indignation back in upon
himself. "No doubt," he says to himself, "it was mostly your
fault—er, no, I mean, mostly *my* fault. If I had acted differently, it never would have happened." Oceans of abuse are

poured on himself. In this suffering he secretly feels superior to less "sensitive" souls, and to some degree is thereby providing an outlet for vindictiveness.

Suffering here serves a much deeper purpose. It is a disguised expression of power on the part of the neurotic's idol. It is first of all a demand: "My intense suffering entitles me to certain rights, privileges and recognitions." Secondly, it is a form of control: suffering is aimed at engendering guilt in others, and the guilty soul will do almost anything to rid himself of feelings of torment. He may even give in and meet the demands of the sufferer. If love and acceptance are returned, they will solve everything. When this purpose is thwarted, the sufferer is even more despondent. In his fantasies he may picture himself dressed in a Japanese kimono, stabbing himself in the market place and dropping his blood-drenched body on the doorstep of his tormentor. Since all doors are closed in the real world, he may fall to pieces in a catastrophic breakdown and give voice to his feelings of hate and vengeance.

It must be reiterated that while this type has gravitated to the despondency pole, he still is in the tri-polar field and under the magnetic influences of both detachment and expansive-vindictiveness. At times he will go away by himself and dream about his mystical fate and the beautiful release that death will one day bring. When he returns to his routine he will seek ways of controlling others by being (not appearing, but *being*) so sweet, co-operative and complimentary that he will be accepted—yea, even considered indispensable—by the powers that be.

If we had accepted the Freudian explanation for this behavior, we would have searched for influences of stringent masochism, sexual satisfaction through suffering, a fixation at the oral-dependence level, and for the instinct of self-destruction. That would have helped us not at all to understand the meaning of suffering for the self-effacing person, and we would have lost sight of the true self that was weakened almost to death but not destroyed. Still less could we understand his behavior when he experiences religious conversion and becomes active in church life.

Previously we mentioned self-surrender as the means of salvation. It seems inevitable that sooner or later this neurotic person will react in a torment of emotional upheaval against tendencies toward the aggressive government of others and toward resignation and detachment. This growing emotional storm comes to a crisis during adolescence, after disappointing experiences with arrogant leaders in peer groups. He experiences guilt over his sporadic expressions of hate and control, frustration over his inability to become a parasite on arrogant persons, torment that his attempted use of sex as a means of "buying" acceptance did not work, and growing fears of loneliness and rejection. Pride is crumbling. Nothing seems to work, and there is no great person to turn to. The cross looms before him as the symbol of eternal grace and infinite love. To many persons involved in this neurotic solution, the cross appears as the answer to their troubles.

Discussing the fascination that arrogance and aggressiveness in others exert on this personality, and his deep need for surrender, Karen Horney makes a remarkable declaration: "We now can see that these two factors are more closely interlinked than we have hitherto realized. He craves to surrender himself body and soul, but can do so only if his pride is bent or broken. In other words the initial offense is not so much intriguing because it hurts as because it opens the possibility for self-riddance and self-surrender. To use a patient's words: 'The person who shakes my pride from under me releases me from my arrogance and pride.' "

The self-effacing personality seizes the cross as the confluence of the emotions that are now interpreted and redeemed by God. Christ is crucified; the neurotic readily admits his complicity in the murder. Pride is shaken; he has failed love and crucified others by his obnoxious vindictiveness. He has tormented the Son of God. But Christ also expresses his own suffering at the hands of others; consequently he identifies himself with the Son of man. As Horney points out, he expects a cure through love. He is prompted "by his hungry expectation that salvation and redemption must and can come only from without . . . through being accepted." That is, when the declaration is made that we are helpless to save ourselves and only the infinite love of God can justify and forgive through the work of the Holy Spirit which is given to us as a gift, then the gospel provides a release that is exquisitely joyful. As a matter of fact, predestination seems not only logical, it is perfectly obvious. At first he doubted that anyone could love *him* that much, but now it is clear. God saved him by infinite love, apart from anything he could do to save himself. The only thing he must do in response is agree to love God with all his heart, and his neighbor as himself. He has no argument with that requirement. It is very clear. This is not *a* way; this is *the* way and Christ is the *Way*.

The Biblical teaching on vicarious suffering seems to him divinely illumined at this point. The neurotic sufferer is an expert when it comes to sympathy. He introjects the experiences of suffering around him. It seems logical to assume, therefore, that the infinite love of God would suffer on account of sin and in behalf of sinful creatures. Furthermore, the suffering Christ continues to love despite claimant rejection. When we identify ourselves with Him in His death and resurrection, we make up what is lacking in the sufferings of Christ. We continue to love and serve others despite persecution. In fact, we are blessed through persecution. We must glory in becoming fools for Christ's sake. He is a Friend who will never leave or forsake us. The believer must decrease that He may increase and give us more of Himself. Love takes no thought of return. Love is for His sake, not especially for the sake of others. Thus the reasoning goes. If this testimony is given at a Wednesday night prayer meeting it is received as the keynote of inspiration. And it comes as no surprise if this testimony is given by a self-sacrificing pillar of the church.

回 回 回

Mr. N. has accepted the "altar call" five times so far this year. Fellow members deplored his going forward to be saved with sinners, but as he said, it was not to be saved. The burdens and turmoil in his soul could only mean that there were pockets of resistance against God somewhere in his life. Self had not been completely erased, for it was obvious he still did not have the peace which passeth understanding. This made sense to the others, but they complimented him on his deep spiritual sensitivity to the presence of sin. Mr. N. seemed to be making progress when one Sunday his pastor's sermon stated that man's true self is not destroyed in Christ but is restored, redeemed and renewed by the Holy Spirit. This confused Mr. N. and he wondered if his minister had not recently been tainted with modernism.

回 回 回

In one sense, the troubles of the neurotic convert are continuing on another plane. The unconscious constellation centering around the function of love has not radically changed. Its base has been widened and shifted. Let us see how this is so.

First, the perfection he sought through loving is now imparted as a gift of the gospel. Moral superiority as a means of

control and a refuge of safety tends to reveal itself more
openly. Surrender to God must surely count for something.
Heaven ought to allow special considerations for special saints.
The prayers of such a saint ought to mean more to God and
to His people. Divine revelation ought to illumine more
Biblical insights for him than for others. His closeness to the
Person of Christ ought to be requited with special preroga-
tives in the life and administration of the church. And he
feels that since God gives freely out of His riches in glory in
Christ, there ought to be no withholding on His part of those
considerations which dishonest and ungrateful creatures too
conveniently forget.

Second, there is confusion over what his love and service
for fellow members entitle him to. On the surface he prefers
to expunge any suggestion that gracious love should be requited. Unconsciously he expects merit and deference in return for gushing concern over the welfare of others.

▣ ▣ ▣

When Mrs. A. heard that the new pastor was coming, she
sent several letters to him introducing herself and explaining
her love and service for the church. She said that she had
cleaned the manse (several others helped) and would see that
the trustees had everything in order when the pastor arrived
with his family. When he did get to the city she came several
times with food for all, and she phoned twice to check that
everything was in good shape. She said that she had a number
of family problems that would call for attention, but she had
no desire to hurry anyone. She would be ready when the dust
settled, so to speak. "Now, if you go out Wednesday or earlier
to visit the shut-ins, and you take your wife, I'll be only too
happy to mind the children. Or I'll visit with you. Feel as
free to call on me as Reverend J. did. Now promise?"

▣ ▣ ▣

The confusion over love depends on the personality structure. Some men, who are thoroughly reliant upon mother, marry, move in to live with mother and treat their wives as boarders. They demand safety and protection and do not know what to do with the contradictory hostility they experience. Then there are others, very active in church affairs, who seek to govern life around them, but who also need assurances of acceptance and appreciation.

For the neurotic who persistently demands tangible assurances of love and acceptance here and now, there tends to be some impatience with the invisible God, and a scurrying to the minister as the church-respected expression of power. In almost every church the pastor can point to one or more persons who tacitly make it clear that their remarkable talents, conversion or history of service endow them with certain inalienable rights, such as the life of the minister, the liberty to do anything in church life, and the pursuit of any position of influence and prestige. Wayne Oates has an apt comment on this point: "On the other hand, other counselees invariably will have severe problems in accepting the pastor as a genuinely human person. They prefer their illusion of his deity. They test his patience and make inordinate demands upon him. They look upon him as the 'one from whom all blessings flow.' They goad his human limitations beyond the point of bearability. In doing so, their own childish desires to be 'god' return to the surface. With many such persons making such demands upon a pastor, he is likely to give way under the strain."

While love is "used" by these persons, they are confused by their own use of it due to their ambiguous demands concerning its requital, or, indeed, whether one has a right to expect any response at all from its object. The idea that God's love is unmotivated by anything in His creatures nourishes the neurotic's notion that there is still much of the fraud in him, and he is not loved for what he is but only because God emits love as freely and compulsively as Yellowstone's Old Faithful emits water. Furthermore, knowing he must love and that he is loved by God, he cannot suppress the resentment that he must keep on loving others while many of them rebuff his designs. This is the core of one of his major conflicts in religious life, and a good example of the reason why neurotic conflicts do not evaporate even though Christ is preached as a God-man revelation to the conflict between a need to be a man and a need to be a god.

This type of disturbed person surrenders himself more deeply and compulsively to God and man, and feels frustrated by both. At the same time he must not permit himself to externalize his self-hate (though in subtle ways he does so). Continuing guilt over self-abuse and signs of outward hostility only serve to fortify his notion of unworthiness. He needs love from a God who loves perfectly when He is loved imperfectly. God keeps on loving plenteously and mechanically, and for the sake of safety and acceptance, the neurotic must do the same. The standards of superiority and prestige in the local church enforce the power of influential persons to accept or reject him on the basis of his advertised claim for recognition and power: continuous, gushing love for everyone.

We have seen that while the game of "King of the Hill" is played with mad abandon, the minister must stand by as the fountainhead of affability. If he has a need to be what Roy Burkhart calls a "love object," he may also capitalize on his appeal as a generous elder brother or as a father image. In any case, he faces the tendency to become a well-mannered robot that smiles mechanically and clasps hands in dutiful reverence before anyone who comes within range and says the key word, "hello."

📧 📧 📧

At the denominational meeting all the pastors were gathered with one or two influential persons from each church. Across the supper table, one minister was conversing with a woman officer from his church. He had learned the technique of eating and smiling at the same time. After every remark of hers, his head nodded soberly and gently, twice, as if moved by a spring. One remark elicited the sweetest joy, and another an expression of profound thought at the revealed wisdom. She remarked that the meat was nice and warm, and he exuded an ineffable radiance of sheer fulfillment. She made the observation that the butter had not been around yet, and he dropped his fork, raised his eyebrows, and was clearly stunned at this collapse of the social amenities. When his poise was restored and the butter found, he continued nodding and smiling until he solemnly bent low to catch another pearl. She commented that they would all burst if they ate another speck, and it was only with the greatest effort that he restrained himself from roaring at her trenchant humor. One could only hope she wouldn't complain of a pain somewhere. Her pastor would be deranged with panic.

📧 📧 📧

The ministry has been recognized as the sphere where some disturbed persons have attempted to reconcile conflicting drives. It is here in the church that love is the answer to their problems. It is here that they must love, regardless of their feelings; where their righteousness will be admired and their rightness respected; where they can defend their leadership and pronouncements by specialized study of a divine Book; where they can ingratiate themselves at the points of human crises, preaching forgiveness in the expectation of being forgiven, and donning the masks of smiling benevolence without appearing to be moronic. To some people, the ministry is a profession specializing in forgiveness. In other areas one might be expected to stand up to expansive-vindictive personalities out to exploit his good nature. Here he is excused from the struggle. You might then expect to find many self-effacing persons with strong trends of morbid dependency in the ministry—and you would find them.

Here again is one of those vicious cycles that is the curse of neurotic disturbances. The more a solid, middle-class Protestant church flees from the spiritual struggle to which Christ's disciples have been commissioned, the more the minister settles down to please persons in the nice affairs and social functions in which they shine, but in which there is neither spiritual fulfillment nor Christian purpose.

"In the ministry today, the on-rush of knowledge and of social change has so eroded the former boundaries of what a minister's central function is, public relations techniques have so much become ends in themselves, social activities have been so emphasized that the task of focusing the minister's activities on those which truly augment his central function and serve his major values has almost been lost sight of. And yet unless the minister, in performing his general function, keeps his central function clearly in mind and his general function definitely subordinated to it, duties are bound to multiply until his central function and the major values it serves are submerged."

This demoralizing process seems to be continuing unabated. Some pastors who are deeply spiritual and quite skilled in their calling examine their inferiority feelings and wonder if they are neurotic, when actually they never visualized themselves as smiling chaplains at an interminable succession of business meetings and high society events. The more each church paves the way for persons striving for social identity through superiority and prestige, the more incumbent it is for the minister to serve this striving with presiding affability, or move on. Mechanical affability in many cases is not an expression of neurosis but a safety device for one unexpectedly thrust into the job of co-ordinator of religious night-life. "Unless he watches closely and resists stoutly, a man can find himself at forty with all his sharp teeth pulled, his nails neatly manicured, his tea manner perfect, his demeanor toward superiors properly deferential, his preaching comfortably consoling but not in the least disturbing, and with twenty-five years more of captivity to go."

The more denominations become organized and autocratic, the more fawning co-operation will be expected by executives from these same pastors. Originally a minister may have felt that he could express his true calling among men ordained to the one ministry of Christ. He discovers that this is not always the case.

Any minister who comes into a church displaying spiritual initiative will be faced with a herculean task. One possible reason why there is a sharp decline in the commitment of students to the gospel ministry is that word may have leaked out that it is precisely the young and aggressive pastors who soon go to have their spirits tried in such churches. No doubt we are enlisting men who have the resources in Christ, the patience, the agility, the training in psychology, and the natural wisdom to follow a morbidly dependent pastor and restore both the ordained and lay ministries to salient spiritual vigor. And doubtless some who are responding to the call have the healthful vitality and prophetic power to break this pattern without succumbing to the temptation to lapse into the ways of a bottled lightning bug. But it is a moot question whether we have enough, and whether they all will be able to stand the strain with inadequate seminary training and almost no practical support from denominational hierarchies.

The neurotically dependent personality can be helped and is being helped. As challenging as his personality structure is, he is a soul before God who needs to be ministered to in the name of Christ. Help will be accepted far more readily than in the case of resigned or extremely aggressive persons. Counseling can and does take place, but care must be exercised that a performance of continuous talking is not misinterpreted by the counselor. The counselor will be circumspect if he senses that he has neither the time nor the training to spend endless hours in strictly nondirective work with a dependent person intent on monopolizing his time. A minister is first of all a loving revealer of God's revelation in Christ. Wayne K. Clymer, Dean of Evangelical Theological Seminary, affirms that the pastor was never meant to be the helpless victim of bookish techniques of nondirective counseling, but that he is under obligation to point out in the appropriate time and way the all-sufficiency of Christ for us sinners.

One of the greatest tasks facing the church is to structure ways for the pastor to receive help. The signs that he is in a predicament are not hard to spot. A *modus vivendi* with a ruling expansive-vindictive group may take the form of servile obedience as the "perfect pastor" who dashes out day or night to their homes in cases of a sprained toe or a slight cough, or who puts into immediate effect their slightest suggestion.

Since neurotic dependence often has a strong sexual coloring, the minister may be magnetized to a sympathetic woman who judges his enemies from his friends for his benefit. Feelings of guilt over such a relationship can only inflame anxiety past the danger point. The trouble is not that the minister is unaware of his need, but rather that he is not sure to whom he can turn. He usually determines to leave or seek help when his inner turmoil places an impossible burden on his wife.

In any successfully therapeutic work the self-effacing person sees that his dependent behavior has been thrown slavishly at the world to satisfy the demands of the perfectly sweet idol. He is confused over love, and makes impossible demands in response to love. If the responses are not what he bargained for, he feels rejected and abused.

One of the jewels of Biblical interpretation is the exegesis of Galatians 5 in *The Interpreter's Bible*: "There are three elements in Paul's love (agape) for his neighbor: esteem for him, desire to help him, and desire for his love in return. These elements also constitute God's love for man as revealed in Christ Jesus."

Healthy Christian love has a right to expectations in response to the outgoing nature of itself. "Paul's Christian race was inspired and enabled by God's grace through Christ, but Paul had to do the running; and if God and Paul's neighbors had withheld the responding love for which he longed, they would have been just as selfish in withholding as Paul in desiring it. They would have loved Paul, not for what he was in himself, but for the service he could render them. The notion that love requires the willingness of the lover to annihilate himself for others is a caricature of Paul's conception."

As we have also seen, the neurotic personality carries over his understanding of human nature to the nature of God. That is, he is confirmed in his dire opinion of love as a useful tool if he continues in the cynical assumption that God's love is unmotivated by anything whatsoever in the saints. To this point the comment is made: "One-sided emphasis on God's love as 'unmotivated' by anything in His creatures tempts men to regard Him in the light of an egotistical philanthropist who expects gratitude and praise but neither needs nor desires the mutuality that is inherent in the very nature of love. . . . Without a faith that dares humbly to believe that God needs man's love, and that He has made man's service an integral part of His infinite enterprise of creation, the Christian's conception of his high calling to be a kingdom builder is liable to reduce itself to blind obedience to commands given arbitrarily for man's good while awaiting God's eschatological fiat. . . . The three elements of agape—esteem, devotion, and mutuality—are present in this fruit of the Spirit, both in God's love for Paul and Paul's love for God."

In therapy we would express the neurotics' goals thus: "love"—a chain holding the sufferers in servile subjection to an idol—left them prey to those who took advantage of their self-surrender; *now,* love must be genuine in an atmosphere of mutuality as it roots itself deeply in faith in God and faith in the self to be a loveworthy creation. The Spirit of God enables them to explore the length and breadth of their humanity, and they must experience God's judgment without discarding themselves as cheap counterfeits of true discipleship. Only as they accept their humanity with its limitations and opportunities can they appropriate the riches of God's grace in Christ.

Whatever else the pastor does for the compliant person, he must be able to absorb bitterness when the compliant person expresses it. If he idolizes the minister and is one of his strong right arms in the church, it may be extremely difficult for the shepherd to accept criticism, especially when he was just beginning to think pretty highly of himself. If hostility is not absorbed, the neurotic may distort true therapy by assuming that he needs acceptance more than ever. Yes, he does need to be accepted for himself, but not in the manner he supposes. He may assume he is accepted only because he encourages peace at any price and because he does exactly right all the favors that the church and minister "require" of him. He has never tested the experience of being accepted for himself, even when he tells God, the minister and the congregation that sometimes he has no use for any of them. He assumes that only *part* of him can be accepted; namely, the part that is sweet and loving, kind and obsequious.

But what about his feelings of intolerance, hate, suspicion, envy and self-rejection? Are they also part of him? As long as he is unable to recognize that they are, he cannot be truly accepted as a person for himself. When he does express them, when he is able to be judged by God without withdrawing, when he is able to taste anxiety and face it without being defeated by it, when positive feelings emerge at the same time as the conflicting hostile ones, then he is coming to grips with his true being. His real self can assert its life because in every sense of the term he is truly being accepted by God.

After counseling a man for a year, the following was part of one session:

🝙 🝙 🝙

Mr. N.: Everywhere I turn, I find people do not express their confidence in me as they used to. I have the feeling of being—well, cut off, you might say.

Pastor: You aren't a bit happy that you are not as close to people as you once were. You sometimes—

Mr. N.: Oh, I don't mean from everyone. Most everybody is nice enough. I mean the very spiritual people. Now that I have dropped the men's association and official board, they—well, I guess they feel I'm a phony, that all the while my heart really wasn't in it.

Pastor: It seems that you—

Mr. N.: Do you know, I think they're saying to themselves that good old —— was just doing it to be a real good Joe and that he's no more religious than the man in the moon. Do you think they're saying that?

Pastor: Well, I don't know what they may be saying. But you feel that they don't think much of you now that you aren't as busy as a bee.

Mr. N.: Yes. Of course, I don't have much to go on. Maybe everyone feels the same. But sometimes I feel out of place. It could be my imagination—it could be me, I suppose. I mean, now that the Lord has put me on the shelf a while, I wonder what use inactive people are to the Lord. But I'll tell you that you try to keep us busy, Pastor. I don't mean to be rude, you understand, but we're supposed to run around with our heads cut off all week, sleep down in the basement so we won't waste time going home and back, just to keep the pot boiling so you can brag you have a very active and spiritual church. Who ever told you that a good church is one in which the people are supposed to sleep in the basement?

Pastor: You mean, just because some people try to keep the minister happy doesn't mean God thinks they are the most lovable, most spiritual persons in the church?

Mr. N.: I guess I'm not being very kind—you know what I think of you, Pastor, you're a wonderful man of God. But well, I guess we're all human, and you try to do your job, and I have mine. But maybe God is just as happy with us when we—I can't express myself so well, but what I'm trying to say is that I know that I'm God's child, even if I don't serve on the boards and all that this year.

Pastor: You're not sure of what you should and should not be doing, but you do seem convinced that God isn't going to punish you or reward you according to how much you please or displease the church. I suppose you could say that God doesn't save our record, He saves *us*.

Mr. N.: (long pause) Sometimes I've felt like a man hanging on a cliff-edge by his fingertips, calling to the people that pass by. Not often, but lately. I don't suppose I have really been happy being so active in the church these past years. But I'm sure God has a place for me in His Kingdom work. I'm sure of it!

▣   ▣   ▣

In this interview Mr. N. quickly covered over his indictment of the minister, but he did express himself and he did feel better about it. And no doubt the minister (in this case, myself) went home and wondered if he really did feel prouder of himself when more people were running around as if their "heads were cut off."

Mr. N. was also under the strong influence of expansiveness. Through the pastor he could keep in everyone's good graces and be the power behind the throne. When his own idol began to topple, he stopped idolizing others and did not think of the church as having a "throne" of power here on earth. This whole therapeutic process went on for many more months, but he came to respect people in the sense that he accepted them whether or not they had a reputation for being influential. As he took in more and more of life, life gave more and more of itself to him.

We have been concerned about the method of training church groups to accept persons by absorbing their feelings. Too often each person wants only to present his own image and viewpoint, without regard for the true feelings of others. We have had some success by conducting a therapy workshop for eight weeks prior to Easter. Every Wednesday, after the sermon, the congregation proceeds downstairs to tables and holds small group discussions. The ground rules are stressed often beforehand:

1) Come in a mood completely receptive to the Holy Spirit.

2) Never permit anyone to make speeches or monopolize the discussion on some vague or minor point in theology.

3) Offer your own problems and testimonies of victory without being overly pious; that is, ask, "How will what I am saying help others or myself? Am I saying this to impress them or make them love me?"

4) Remember that one of the Spirit's fruits is joy.

5) Be completely understanding, respectful and sympathetic to the contributions of other persons.

6) Make listening a labor of love. Concentrate intently on what the other person is saying. Try to understand him and his remarks. No matter what he says or calls anyone, listen to him courteously until he is finished. Let any bitterness come out of him into the openness of the group.

7) Don't be afraid of silence. Let silence work for you. If you can't think of anything you want to say aloud, don't speak. God works well in stillness.

8) Don't bring up anything someone else has said here in another time or place. Respect the confidence others place in you. Be a friend others can trust. When someone expresses bitterness to you about yourself or another, pray about it and do not express it to anyone else.

We are assuming here that souls will learn the value of thus being fellow ministers and will carry over this therapeutic work to other groups and relationships. The neurotics may see these group discussions as oportunities to let their glory shine, but the Holy Spirit has other plans. We can afford to be as patient with others as the Spirit is with us.

One word here about bibliotherapy, which applies not only to compliant persons but to all with neurotic trends. I have great faith that God uses the reading of the right book at the right time. Finding those two "rights" may be quite a task, but experience has proved that the risks of an educated guess are almost always worth it.

Occasionally reading an excellent sermon or spiritual book will get a person to thinking. When he says, "Pastor, sometime when you happen to have a free minute, I'd like to discuss So-and-so's thought with you," that usually means "Something here is bothering me and I'd like to talk." If the counselor or discussion group is aware of emotional content, the "talkathons" may turn into a harvest of the Spirit.

We have found that the time after the reaching of a crisis of identity is opportune for finding the right book or sermon. The person on the road to health is not only clearing the debris, he is building. He is exploring with new confidence and vitality, and spiritual ideas are grist for his mill. He is strengthened by the reading of good books. There is no need to make a list. Any pastor can look up in his study and see any number of books for the right time and the right person. But does the church have a small library with a number of books that will fit the bill? We can only hope so, in order that the counselee doesn't feel the minister is judging him harshly or forcing him to one point of view against his will. If we are determined to respect the integrity of any soul to follow the light into health and vigor, we have to be genuinely honest in our resolve.

In a sense, the person living in the psychological realm of the parasite is hard to understand and deal with because his one thought seems to fulfill Scripture: to love his neighbor. He lacks one thing: to fulfill the law of Christ, he has yet to love himself.

6
Journey from Life

WE HAVE SEEN NEUROSIS AS AN ANXIETY-RIDDEN WAY OF LIFE, soaring above dangers real or imagined to heights of glory in fantasy. On this flight the faltering ego threatens to split apart. The neurotic person wants everyone to love or obey him, but he is sure most of them really dislike him. He must be godlike, but he also must be humble. He must be both sides of all coins at the same time.

His solution is entirely unconscious. He is held together by the mold of his idol. His self-image of a self-styled superman permeates his thinking. When you suggest that he is not what he thinks he is, he does not know what you are talking about. He only knows that he *is* all-loving, or all-powerful, or all-wise. When he states that he hopes people will accept him as he is, he means that he will feel safe to the degree that the world accepts his glorious self-image. If he joins the church he takes the idol right in with him, assuming the idol will be Jehovah's right arm. How imperative that he translate neurotic trends into religious terms! How can the world not see how devoted he is to his religion?

At the base of the neurotic mind is, in a sense, a trinity competing with the divine Trinity. This trinity is the tri-polar field we have previously mentioned. One pole is the self-effacing solution of neurotic love, and another is the solution of expansive-vindictiveness, that is, the yearning for unlimited power and glory. At this point we are concerned with the third pole, detachment: the journey from life through independence and resignation.

One can imagine the goals of glorification through love, or mastery over others. But how can anyone worship independence? Independence from what? To what? By what means? What does this person do—travel to a far-off island, live like Robinson Crusoe, and thank God that he is governor, council and total population of his tight little kingdom?

When you think about it, flight does seem the first logical response to danger. If a hungry lion charged you in darkest Africa, the first suggestion you would entertain is, "Let's *go!*" The unconscious mind thinks that way. It may also be led to believe that the world is darkest Africa, with ferocious lions lurking in every shadow, and the safest soul is the one who keeps a canyon between himself and the beasts. Once you grant a few of these premises about life, you have a pretty good case for the ensuing logic.

When the detached person was a child, he often felt helplessly at the mercy of several notable lions. He had little confidence in his power to overcome them or appease them. Usually he had to shoulder an extreme burden placed upon him by parents, either in the form of too much work ("Idle hands get into mischief") or demands too high to be met. We find parents with neurotic trends making excessive demands of scholastic attainment or outstanding social or athletic performance which the children must meet to avoid humiliation and alienation. Such a child realizes, "I can only barter with the world with the coins of moral aloofness and outstanding competence."

Parents with excessive and morbidly rigid moral codes "work out" their conflicts through children and demand that they be extremely cautious around anything that smacks of sex or too much enjoyment. The child grows up feeling lost to himself and humiliated, and yet he must work like a

·113·

demon to measure up to parental demands for which he lacks the inner confidence.

"The accusation against society appears in two forms. It either states: 'I have not got the position, influence and reputation that I deserve; I have been cheated out of my just deserts; I have not had a chance to develop in accordance with my gifts; I am one of the disinherited.' Or it states the very opposite: 'Too much is demanded of me; I am good for nothing; I am capable of nothing; I am a zero.' And the deeper the investigation penetrates these attitudes, the clearer it becomes that these two apparently contradictory accusations exist side by side."

Under these conditions the "we-someness" (Fritz Kunkel) of life is lost and the victim feels his position is hopeless. Of course, he pushes himself that much harder to avoid guilt, and the more he pushes the more he resents the pushers. Since any expression of hostility is out of the question, he punishes himself by working still harder.

When the inevitable revolt takes place, little by little or all at once, the person cannot return to re-satellization. The paradox of self-surrender and independence is not handled satisfactorily. The breakaway from those who make demands through the offering of love or great responsibility is final, while the need for dependence is deeply repressed. The mind has apparently "found itself" at last. Its philosophy is rigid: "Tell the whole world to jump in the lake!"

What is the idol that rules this soul? It is the idol of splendid isolation—I call it "safe, silent superiority." If we must have some picture in our minds, imagine a smiling god looking down from Olympia. Let us examine this "god" to see what he thinks.

First, he feels his distance from the whole of life. He is in the world but not of it. Invisible hands reached into his heart and turned off vital emotions as one would turn off a spigot. In counseling he complains that he "just doesn't feel a thing" for his father, or brother, or wife, or anyone. It is as if he went cold when the pressure got too great, and he is no longer involved in life because he doesn't *feel* life. Immediate family members often sense that he comes and goes almost with indifference, as if a little steel wall surrounded his heart, and no one ever gets to him.

Next, he feels safe, and superior to others. How does he manage that? He does it by making perfection even more perfect. He makes a little deal with life. He will do what is expected at the job. A certain number of required tasks will be done at home. He will be externally moral until it hurts. He will smile, be benevolent; he will never raise his voice, lose his temper, or act nasty. He will pay his bills, avoid skirmishes with neighbors, and take the children out for a ride once a week. He will be known as "one swell guy" and "a real ace if there ever was one." He will be quietly sagacious, and the higher his I.Q. the safer he feels.

And what will life do for him in return? It is very simple. Life will keep its distance. It will not hurt, make undue demands, or pressure him into a corner. If it does, it will be unfair. Thus, as in all neuroses, the claims are evident. In this case the claim is that life should not hurt him and people should not bother or endanger him.

Superiority, however, depends on more than this. It is measured not only by his height above others, but also by their distance below him. The god of splendid isolation lays a strong foundation of safe, silent superiority by carefully cataloguing the faults of others. His careful eye is trained to perfection in the art of observing the flaws and transgressions of those about him. He thus has an airtight case against them. He may never use the evidence, but his memory is good. He has the satisfaction of "knowing the score" on other poor mortals.

🔲 🔲 🔲

The woman sat back in the chair, relaxed. "I'm not worried a bit," she confided. "My husband was supposed to take a client out, but I called the office when he should have been back, and there was no answer. I called again at—oh, roughly, 7:38 P.M., and there was still no answer. If that's the way he is, that's perfectly all right with me. But I've had it. And he'd better not boss me around or tell me what to do any more. I won't bother him, and I certainly don't expect him to bother me."

🔲 🔲 🔲

If he lets his fantasy run riot, the detached personality would picture himself as a great eagle soaring above the plains. Or, he would be the only observer above the field of life on which everyone is playing a furious game of football. They are involved, but he looks on from above. He sees their mistakes and knows how the game should be played. He sees all the fools hurting themselves, and he even gets a kind of vicarious satisfaction from watching the pathos of victory or defeat. He may come down and visit the field, but always as an observer. He can discuss himself with a scientific detachment, as if he were giving a discourse on someone living in another world. He may even enjoy "the sight of himself" enjoying himself at a party, thrilling to a sexual situation with a woman, or giving the sales department a pep talk. The complete self-surrender of love, however, is entirely out of the question. That is a booby trap to be avoided at all costs, though in half the cases he would say, "Why, sure, if the right person came along I could be happy." He seems to sense that once you begin to love someone, or get into her debt, she has a hold on you. No, that must *never* be! "What is your definition of love?" he asks, in the spirit of philosophical speculation.

In matters of religion we find the detached personalities filling the whole spectrum of religious dedication. Some have a touch of religion, or, as we shall see with "the Pharisee," some may be preoccupied with religion every waking hour. On the whole, there are formidable barriers in the path of their deep-rooted dedication to Christ as Lord of life.

First of all, many persons of this type have run through stages of compliance and independence, satellization and rebellion, and they are now firmly dedicated to a rejection of any forms of self-surrender. They see nothing but danger in throwing their souls to something or someone outside their control.

Second, their obsession with intellectual explanations bars the door to faith. They are suspicious of faith, hope and love, and prefer the observation post to the mourner's bench. None are so "secure" as those who tie life's enigmas in a sophisticated explanation and put them up on the shelf with the other homemade remedies for which they have little use. The acute and chronic unbelief that discards religion as a mythical folk nostrum is often a suspicious rebellion against the self-surrender that is the requisite for creative rapport among souls.

Third, there is a rejection here of what may be considered an intensification of legalistic bondage. Churches in some of the large midwestern cities often encounter numerous families from small ultra-conservative churches in rural areas. They come to the Big City for freedom, but they remain deathly afraid of going to any church. Their conflict becomes patent when they say, "If we went to any church, it would be one like the small one back home, but right now we don't feel like going to any." The prodigal son, incidentally, probably couldn't decide which he felt was more distasteful, the rigid rectitude of his father or the cold self-righteousness of his brother. The background does leave its mark. We have spoken to some great sinners who suddenly had profound, soul-shaking religious conversions. It often comes out that mother was a strict religionist or father was a lay preacher. Although there is often a Pauline self-surrender under the guilt of a punitive law's condemnation from youth, it is not always involved in conversions of this color.

Fourth, detached persons value their privacy so much that they evade the interference of a loving God. Horney once remarked: "Any question put to him about his personal life may shock him; he tends to shroud himself in a veil of secrecy. A patient once told me that at the age of forty-five he still resented the idea of God's omniscience quite as much as when his mother told him that God could look through the shutters and see him biting his fingernails."

Small groups and fellowship meetings often indulge in frank confessions and expressions of the need for personal prayer. Such warmth and intimacy frighten the detached personality.

Fifth, he rejects the idea that his own moral attainment is so inadequate that God in Christ suffered for his transgressions. He prefers to feel that his righteousness has won him independence from God. This symptom differs from the defensiveness of unredeemed persons in that the neurotically compulsive nature of the moral facade makes unthinkable his descent to the level of all sinners.

Sixth, this type of person is living on the basis of safe, *silent* superiority. He quietly and secretly gloats over the knowledge of the sin and hypocrisy of so many churches and their people. The very suggestion of becoming a part of that which he de-

·118·

fends himself against—the alleged superior righteousness of the churches—is too fraught with anxiety.

Seventh, he is easily hurt, and when he is, his first thought is to resign or run away. Self-hate is experienced for not measuring up to his own standards. He punishes himself, and externalizes his self-hate. He assumes others do not like him and are attempting to coerce him. He is suspicious. When tempted to revert to compliance, he is especially susceptible to rejection or even to being taken for granted. When he feels that the minister has rejected him, his position is jeopardized and he runs from the scene of battle to sulk. Every person in church work has run into several individuals who run in Christian circles like a fireman's team of horses dashing off to the fire, and who, after they get burned, run to pout in jittery seclusion. This whole group, and compliant persons who have been slighted, contribute liberally to the body of "church tramps," who visit churches as some take in theaters.

There are essentially two reasons why the detached personality indulges in some nominal religion at all. In numerous cases the guilt of divorcing himself completely from church attendance is too much to cope with if his parents had insisted on attendance. If, however, the authority of church is associated too strongly with parental authority, the adolescent rejection of church life may be inexorable.

Another reason why he may dabble in religion is to patronize the church. If the church in any given area is firmly established as the symbol of rightness, then it enhances his godlike qualities to impart a blessing to struggling mortals by his attendance at worship.

One can immediately get a taste of the shallowness of this neurotic solution. It has raised cynicism to the nth degree and covered it with a social veneer of pleasant condescension. No doubt it appears easy to be cynical of love in western civilization. Love is something that makes us psychotic, according to our songwriters. Love writes our commercials, inspires our cosmetic firms, grinds out our TV dramas in partnership with violence, cuts out our fashions, emboldens our heroes, consoles our cowards. It is the reason for marriage, the excuse for adultery and the scapegoat for divorce. Everyone loves love and sentimentalizes passion. We long to be carefree, beautiful, and dashing in order to be loved, as if love were the first and only prize in a desperate beauty contest.

The detached person considers himself too shrewd to be taken in by this sham. In an age shattered by insecurity and threatened with extinction, he is not going to rush out into the storms of unrequited yearning, jealousy, betrayal and disappointment in search of an elusive pot of gold at the end of the rainbow. He is going to play it safe. He will play life like a game of chess, with his eyes open and planning well ahead.

And where will it all lead? What is there to look forward to? I shall never forget a counselee suddenly looking up with a blank expression on her face and calmly announcing, "I wish I were dead." In such a moment of nothingness, surely the gospel must have some appeal. Surely it must reach out and somewhere in the dark recesses of the heart strike a spark of hope. Of course it does! Time after time we have heard a person who has erected a great wall between himself and life testify to a soul-shattering conversion—their waking hours now are seldom filled with any thought but that of pleasing God. Down through the ages this type of individual has found his place among the most seriously dedicated religionists. How is it that some in this group have no stability in religion, while others give their lives to it? What is the appeal to the latter segment?

There is the appeal of release. It is release from the torment of moral insufficiency in the face of righteous requirements impossibly above us. "Wretched man that I am! Who will deliver me from this body of death?" Guilt is like a noose that tightens every day. To be freed from it is to run into the vistas of a whole new life.

There is the appeal of righteous imputation. Righteousness "will be reckoned to us who believe in him that raised from the dead Jesus our Lord. . . ." This means that the whole gospel is directly concerned with that which the detached person is too terrified to face; namely, the inability of a human being to be perfect. The neurotic agrees (though for the wrong reason) that perfection is still desired. God in His infinite love gives the truly repentant person the benefit of the doubt, and imputes to his account a standing of absolute rightness and unity with Himself through the graciously imparted merits of our Redeemer.

There is the appeal of love *from a distance*. The detached person would not be afraid of love if it could possibly be perfect and never too close for comfort. That is the way he sees the infinite love of God. God accepts us, but will not betray us. We can open our hearts to Him without fear of exploitation. His love is unalloyed by any evil intent. His love is devoid of any sexual coloring. His love is from heaven and not as close or as "material" as parents or a married partner. A move of reconciliation with the fact of love seems a happy prospect after many years of emptiness. The detached person hears that infinite love is offered from a perfect Being, without prior conditions or merit or attainment. He likes what he thinks he hears.

Lastly, there is the appeal of reconciliation with an estranged father. We have previously noted the anxiety of parents that their legalistic codes should be incarnated in their children. The rebellion of children usually means their estrangement from parents. In cases where one or both parents were hateful or indifferent, the estrangement is still a fact, even though repressed. The Bible states that we are reconciled to God. We have returned home from rebellion and are received by the open arms of our Father. When the person who has been victimized by his own "distance machinery" (Harry Stack Sullivan) partakes of this reconciliation, it is no wonder to him that the gospel is called "good news."

No doubt many Christians will sense that, on the face of it, the gospel seemed to appeal to them for similar reasons. Does that mean we are all neurotic? Hardly. The generalization would be as senseless as saying that all church squabbles are aggravated by the influences of deeply disturbed persons. But there is no doubt that neurotic defenses are close at hand for most of us. Who has not been wounded and vowed that he would never trust people again? Who has not decided to turn his back on tomorrow because his fondest dreams crumbled to ashes? That the perfect Judge proved His faith in us by sending His Son to die and rise from the dead for our sins, is an appeal the Holy Spirit can make to all mankind. This is a catholic gospel, and it meets the conditions of all men in all ages.

The horizontal plane in the tri-polar field between the neurotic solutions of detachment and expansive-vindictiveness is monopolized by a defensive system which we may call "pharisaism." Any point on this plane leaning toward one solution more than the other can be accompanied by symptoms invested with varying shades of religious dedication, and may be evidenced in any church of any theological disposition. As it is commonly employed, the term "pharisaism" can mean any degree of spiritual pride. The term here means a condition of neurotic pride heavily weighted with the defensive mechanisms of safe, silent superiority. Expansive-vindictiveness is present to some degree, and the personality is characterized by an anxious determination to maintain a select position of respected superiority in the presence of religious persons who maintain due regard for that position.

The pharisee creates an idol that is a projection of himself, and he worships it. Thereafter, this idol is in competition with the true and living God, although the idolator feels that he is in such complete accord with God that they are in perfect harmony. On the surface he seems to reject the praise of worshipers, but is watchful for the envy of other pharisees who may be in competition with him.

I will use a parable to illustrate. Picture a tower high on a hill. The tower is massive, lofty and impregnable. Periodically a kingly-looking person of quiet, regal demeanor leaves the tower and descends to the valley of the common folk. He mixes with them in a spirit of polished good humor and fatherliness. He pats some on the head, encourages others, and after a number of fervid requests from the masses, gives one or two quiet lectures on the awful sinfulness of sin. When his advice is requested on the depths of profound ethical questions—such as, "Should we drink coffee? Is it a sin to go to the movies? Is the modern dance the main cause of juvenile delinquency?"—he lifts his eyes to heaven in ill-suppressed exasperation at the blindness of these people "cursed without the law," and drops a few spiritual pearls for them to treasure. There is no question in anyone's mind that not one wit is he tainted by coffee, cigarettes, movies, or the dance, but of course they certainly appreciate his patience with those who have not yet come into the light.

This ultraholy king is a hail-fellow-well-met with obvious

sinners. He can laugh with the best of them, and is considerate enough to listen attentively to the recitation of the transgressions of others from the lips of aspiring pharisees and devoted admirers. His good deeds somehow have a way of getting noised abroad to every corner of the domain, but it is clear that he wants no credit for them. Whatever good he does is not for others but for God (god). Others don't deserve it.

As everyone is supposed to know, this king of rightness does not wish to appear perfect. He *is* perfect. Like the poor preacher of *The Scarlet Letter,* his confessions of sinfulness only enhance the respect of the masses for his piety.

After the descent, the king returns to the pinnacle, his spiritual ivory tower, affectionately dubbed in his unconscious, "The Mount of Transfiguration." Up there it is lonely but safe. The emptiness of the castle and the echoing barrenness of the bare walls are part of the price gifted persons must pay for their exalted positions. Envy stalks the corridors at night, but he is banished by a review of the secret sins of the poor rabble below. Life at the Holy Land Estates is hollow and cold, but it is safe. Above all, *it is safe.* And if the crowd below seems to be enjoying itself it is only because the crowd doesn't know any better. They will all cry in hell.

This life could continue forever, but let us suppose that one day the king descends and encounters one or two visiting prophets who have evidently strayed too far from their own estates. They point out some of *his* mistakes and have the ultrapious lives to back up their claims for attention. They may even resort to the foulest blow of all and remark that the king is self-righteous. The people are fascinated by this observation and rather taken up with the newcomers.

The king from the tower smolders with almost uncontrollable rage. Almost, yes—but he must not lose his temper.

He may get ulcers, perilous changes in blood pressure, feelings of drowsiness, palpitations of the heart, indigestion, heartburn, muscle cramps, pains around the neck and upper back, or migraine headaches—but he does not "fly off the handle."

Now what to do? He returns to the tower to plan his strategy. The pharisaic king must proceed, he is certain, from the premise that the intruder who criticized him is, *ipso facto,* a fraud. He is unquestionably a great sinner out for the approval and control of the masses. The fact that the people are taken up with him only proves they must be saved from their own spiritual blindness. The decision is made to lie in patient wait until this pious fraud tips his hand and reveals his hypocrisy. Perhaps he can be trapped into doing so, to save time.

The pharisee bides his time and makes a mental note of anything that can be construed as evidence in the case against his opponent. If the opponent is an ordained minister the task is simplified because he takes the leadership before the eyes of the public. One observation after another is recorded by the pharisee. There seems to be nothing earthshaking in any one fault, but with just the right interpretation—and putting them all together—well, they make quite a case. Especially relished are the sins of which the pharisee claims he is not guilty. As the list grows it includes such items as: not a bit patient with old persons, too abrupt with young people, spends too much time in the garden, too controversial on some points of theology, crosses legs awkwardly when seated behind the pulpit, is lax in some cases of visitation to shut-ins, at times dresses much too informally, brings the wrong kind of people into the church, did not fully co-operate with officers in following their orders in several flagrant cases, puts too much emphasis on counseling, set up a program and used the film projector without consulting the elder associated with that sort of thing for years, has too many children, uses slang, is known to play cards, and (repeated because of its great importance) is not very tactful.

If the competitor does make a gross mistake, the kingly pharisee's troubles are over. The cat is out of the bag. The sanctity of the realm has been vindicated at last!

If all the items listed above do not bear enough weight, the pharisee is not above coloring them with a few clashing shades. By the time these revelations reach the second or third reporter, the story may be an outright lie. In the mind of the mythical king this is entirely justified. He feels that he has the perception to see through the enemy, but the poor masses do not, and the painting must be touched up to give them the true picture. This type of disturbed person may be accepted according to his claims for years, until he is forced to justify specious ends with flagrant means in order to preserve a position he considers threatened. In any case, no peace is ever signed with the enemy, for the simple reason that he has not made a peace with his true being.

Something must eventually give. The pharisee will leave the scene of battle like a martyr, to live in splendid but ever more tormented isolation, or he may be prepared to struggle forever. It depends on which point in the tri-polar field exerts the strongest magnetism: detachment or expansive-vindictiveness. If the enemy does leave, the pharisee plunges into the furious task of mending fences and restoring confidence in the status quo.

If this parable clarifies anything, it shows us that safety is equated with rightness in the mind of this neurotic. If the compliant type worships an image of love, and the expansive-vindictive person an image of power, the pharisee worships his definition of rightness. Rightness, as defined by a religious code, is a convenient method of winning approval from a large number of people who have professed respect for it. The listing of external criteria for rightness and wrongness is a verifiable method of testing the status of persons in a religious community dominated by legalism. It is a simplified method of demonstrating what the congregation (rewarding audience) can see and evaluate. This method serves to elevate those who fervently work at it and places in their proper places of submissiveness those who are remiss.

The second point this parable accentuates is the underlying current of rage. It is rage directed at outside threats, and inwardly at the sufferer for permitting himself to be ruffled by the threat. Self-hate is externalized so that the pharisee grows in his conviction that his competitors are out to annihilate him. The rightness of his position can only be vindicated by an utterly glorious defeat of his foes.

Rightness, however, does not have to be established on the basis of ethics alone. In our churches it can be fortified by more formal education, a Ph. D., forty years of service in the congregation ("No one knows this church like I do!"), or a dedication to preserving the fine points of denominational doctrine. Some Christians are so determined to uphold the inspiration of every line of Scripture that their time is devoted to defending and studying it without giving a serious thought to its teachings on humility and compassion.

Donald Macleod speaks of the unfortunate tendency in most American churches for the choir and its director to become a professional order that vies with the clergy for attention, prominence and congregational preferment, and so it appears that rightness may also be fortified by professional competence. Occasionally these tensions get out of hand. If the choir director is disturbed by neurotic trends of pharisaism, the pastor has a real problem on his hands. The director contends that he has as much specialized competence in his field as the minister has in his. The pastor may feel that an armed truce is unchristian but preferable to invading a guarded domain, even if this caution means stifling his initiative and the imaginative program a partnership could inspire.

Trends of pharisaism in the pastor are quite repressed. It may be possible for him to coast for years on the notion that the undershepherd is a little deity and his pulpit the temple. If he runs head-on into the neurotic trends of certain pillars of the church he may decide that half a loaf is better than none, and that it is better to be the unquestioned head of part of a congregation than to wear a shaky crown in all the church.

◫　◫　◫

Reverend David B. came to the Green Meadows Church in June, 1952. He made many changes in the first five months and encouraged a forward-looking program in all phases of church life. He requested the organist to look for a choir director, feeling that one person could not do both tasks. He requested the official board to change the church secretary. She was a member of the church. He asked the Christian education committee to review the work of the teachers in the adult education department, and particularly to interview Mr. J. who had been teaching the Berea Class for eleven years. Mr. J. resigned.

One month later, Reverend B. discussed with Mr. J. the teaching of the senior-high class. Mr. J. stated that he did not agree with the minister's views on the coming of Christ and the world tribulation of the last days. The pastor became angry as the discussion continued, and insisted that as a scholar and specialist in this field his views should take precedence. Mr. J. coolly replied that after eleven years he had learned a few things himself.

By the end of the year, the organist, church secretary and Mr. J. were meeting regularly to exchange notes concerning the minister who "was slowly ruining their church." The minister heatedly demanded that the board go on record supporting his views in eschatology. The board was divided on the grounds that this was not the heart of the problem.

The pastor next called a congregational meeting and requested a vote of confidence in his Biblical scholarship and teaching ministry. The hostility which came out during the meeting left the pastor stupefied. The next day he wrote a letter to the congregation, announcing his resignation and calling on all true supporters of the Biblical view of the pretribulation rapture and premillennial return of Christ to arise as a testimony to the glory of God. They would meet in the Community Hall and hold services there as a purified church. Thirty-five per cent of the congregation took out their membership and a new church was formed.

Now, several years later, no one can adequately explain what the separation was about. Some persons claimed that Mr. J. confided the minister had to leave over "a moral issue," but would not elaborate. Apparently to most it was a doctrinal issue, but most of the members of both churches confided to friends that they weren't quite sure what the pretribulation rapture meant. At any rate, Mr. J. is teaching the Berea Class and Reverend B. is still pastor of the new church, although it took in only 125 new members since it was formed.

▣ ▣ ▣

In this history, the minister strengthened his position in his own mind by an intensive survey of books favoring dispensationalism. Since he was sure he was right, his opponents were absolutely wrong. He supported his splitting of the church on the basis of II Corinthians 6:17: "Therefore come out from them, and be separate from them, says the Lord. . . ." To other pastors who discussed the problem with him he replied, "It is better to have a small church pure in spirit than a large church without a knowledge of the Word of God." He never showed any signs of uncovering his unconscious need to withdraw, to vindicate a position of rightness, to rationalize interpersonal conflict on the basis of doctrine, or to externalize his self-hate by blaming Mr. J. for an obstinate refusal to accept God's Word. He never showed any insight into the fact that he could not play god except before a totally appreciative audience. His memory was colored with rage in the thought that Mr. J., the organist and the secretary had won a victory of sorts. "Why they even acted like the Pharisees," he consoled himself.

It is strange that who the original Pharisees ("separated ones") were, and what they believed, concerns us so little, especially when the question occupies so much of the New Testament. Actually, they belonged to one of three sects, and numbered more than six thousand during the reign of the Herods. They managed to get a majority in the Sanhedrin, and claimed they embodied in their writings and behavior the oral law explaining the Law of Moses. Dr. William Smith writes that they ". . . sought mainly to attract the attention and to excite the admiration of men."

The sect built a world of their own in which they stood aloof as the guardians of the Law and the chosen of the chosen. Their platform of pride was constructed of adherence to hundreds of vexatious and trifling extensions of the Ten Commandments, prescribing how one should bathe, fast, wash cups, conduct one's self on the Sabbath, and on and on. The Pharisees clearly indicated, in an age of status-seeking and insecurity, how neurotic persons can take the values of the world into the community of faith and build around themselves an appreciative audience that vitiates the community. The rest of this community of faith, for all its good points, became nourished by neurotic values of superiority and prestige, fed into itself the poisons of suspicion and back-biting, suffocated the Scriptural teachings of faith, love and justice by its harsh legalism, and eventually fell into the hands of disturbed men ravaged by their own vindictiveness.

The Pharisees had no trouble in erecting barriers of superiority against the people until Jesus arrived. Jesus was considered by them to be an uneducated upstart. He did not hesitate, however, to puncture their pride, uncover their defenses, indict their empty formalism, and point them to the fundamentals of true religion: rebirth by God's Spirit, inner holiness, mercy, forgiveness, obedience to God and compassion for man. He made a shambles of their platform by breaking their oral tradition when it contravened the basic law of the spirit of life. And yet, He fulfilled the Law; He did not reject it.

How could the Messiah elevate these men to glory and still be a poor Carpenter? Never! He uncovered their own lust for money, power and prestige, and they experienced intense guilt. Their self-hate was turned on Him as the cause of their troubles. He reduced them to the level of the masses and He was a suitable target for the vindictiveness they had been gathering for years. Every pharisaic guardian of the sanctity of the domain badly needs a righteous cause and a red-hot battle. The ancient Pharisees knew from the start that the Carpenter was a worthy target for their holy hate. At first they attempted to guard their actions before the masses, but the people were blind, so any means justified their ends. Nothing but the sight of Christ's blood trickling to the sun-baked earth could temporarily satisfy their vindictive wrath.

Today pharisaism is not limited to any one sect in any one area ministering to one particular economic stratum. It can be a rampant malignancy in our ultrafundamentalist churches. Over the years one can observe a congregation drive out healthy personalities and attract to itself a host of detached persons vying sedulously with one another in an external morality of personal abstinence. The whole atmosphere becomes bathed with the spirit of the Gestapo. At the Wednesday night prayer meeting, everyone contributes a polished testimony of personal victory in a game of "Can You Top This?" Announcement that So-and-so is absent and needs prayer for a secret request often means "How the mighty have fallen!" Gossip about members is cloaked in a concern for their full sanctification. Bible scholars in the pew are on guard lest the pastor skirt the truth.

And nothing is more pathetic than to observe a pharisaic pastor struggling to maintain peace at any price by out-phariseeing the pharisees. One's thoughts turn to Paul's plea: "For the whole law is fulfilled in one word, 'You shall love your neighbor as yourself.' But if you bite and devour one another take heed that you are not consumed by one another."

One cannot infer that ultrafundamentalism alone breeds neurotic pharisaism. Much of Protestant modernism was a separation from the historic faith on the basis of the trend of mastery through perfection and intellectual superiority. For many it was a disgrace to associate with a creed-worn "fanaticism." Being somewhat self-conscious about their obvious trending toward superior aloofness, they professed the urge to "return the church to the laymen." At the same time they began donning religious costumes and instituting contrived liturgy to widen the breach between themselves and the poor occupants of the pew.

Among ultraliberal pastors there are outspoken proponents of tolerance for anything and everything. But they betray a fuming rebellion by lashing vehemently against all things evangelical, and somehow insist that those who uphold the historic doctrines of the church are not true to their denomination! One can only imagine what is in the hearts of pastors throughout the nation who have been persecuted by an ultraliberal minor official in the denomination for allegedly being a "Bible-pounding fundamentalist from the hills."

When whole churches and sects become neurotic it is interesting to note how disturbed persons attract their own kind. This is especially true of detached personalities. The pharisees may be suspicious of each other and keep each other at a distance, but there is a kind of "honor" among them. Each finds personal safety and a subtle satisfaction in keeping a private file of the others' sins. But there is the need for a greater impact of a strict legal code on the masses. The exclusiveness of the elect club grows more impressive if it has enough members to augment the importance of the code before the people. And the pleasure of outdoing other club members is more exquisite than impressing the masses who know no better. Here again, this relationship can exist only if each member has a guarded domain, and the minister supports the key families guarding the rights and privileges of each sector. Anything or anyone who threatens to upset this carefully balanced status-pyramid will find himself the target of a storm of vindictiveness.

Beyond these examples, the great danger today is that the pharisaic person is working feverishly to force the church as an institution to ape the world in its struggle for exclusiveness and superiority based on the status of exalted favor. The church then worships itself as an end in itself. The church provides the altar upon which the world's idols are sanctified for more effulgent prestige.

It is imperative that we know some of the reasons why the church is doing this. The sociological laws for the growth and stability of institutions are not enough, for the church is not just another institution. When we get into the psychological as well as the sociological factors, we note the absence in almost all churches of persons in the eighteen- to twenty-six-year-old bracket. This group suspects that the older persons are frustrated in their attempts to be crashing successes in the world and are now condemning the world while aping its echelons of superiority and prestige; or they are fairly successful in the world and desire divine sanction for their status. In either case the older persons have closeted themselves off from the sins and burning social problems of our time and are busy playing house among themselves. The youth generally feel that the church is a pharisaic fossil from Bible times. If the powers of hell cannot crash the gates of the castle, neither can new ideas or a fresh visitation of the Spirit's power. Up in the towers there is a masquerade party, while down below the world's midnight hour is fast approaching.

What we are concerned with here and now are remedial approaches to the soul resigned from the task of living his true being. Consider first, *the love crisis*. More important than any other remedy is the preparation for the love crisis. The resigned person has made a solitary journey away from his own life. He is closed off from spontaneous being, and has locked love in the closet of isolation and safe, silent superiority. He needs to see that his neurotic solution for his anxiety is really his problem. He needs the strength to come home, and though the return is a lonesome one—and often a terrifying one—it can be lighted by the knowledge of someone to help him home. In extremely severe cases the Christian psychotherapist must help him return. In most cases for the Christian, it will be his pastor.

The blessing of God is upon this person and his pastor sitting alone together, face to face. Sermons and lectures will not do here, because this person is adept at observing himself with a detachment that disdains change. There seems to be no emotional lever by which his soul can be prodded. Instead, there must slowly grow the enlightenment that the two souls present are joined together. The counselee is accepted and loved by the counselor. Will he reject the egotistical "I-before-you" in favor of the "spirit of we" which the counselor helps provide? The counselor is not God. He is simply God's agent in assisting the counselee to find himself without outside prodding, directing, psychological lectures, questions, or censures from the Word.

The counselee thinks to himself, "Why don't you judge me when I reveal my weaknesses and hates?"

The counselor is implying: *Because I myself have been judged by God.*

"Why do you listen to the drivel of my confessions?"

Because He has promised that if we go to Him He will not cast us out.

"Why do you love *me*, if you really do?"

Because we are loved by God.

"Why do you not laugh at my pretenses?"

Because both our souls are open before the one cross.

"Why do you not harp on my sins?"

Because we both need the conviction and healing of God's Spirit.

"How can I be sure you will not betray me if I let you into my life?"

Because He has given us eternal life, and no one can snatch

*us out of His hand. Christ is the Light of life. We sanctify
this life in us by reflecting its light to our brethren.*

The counselor needs limitless resources of patience. Gradually the counselee is relieved that the man in front of him is
not God, nor does he pretend to be. He senses that he is not
yielding to the pastor's point of view; he is responding to the
call of his true self. He is not merely accepting the pastor's
acceptance of him; he is not merely accepting himself. He is
accepting the fullness of God's life as the depths of its love
and power become appealing to him.

Perhaps over the years he may slowly make his way back
home. Perhaps he will say, "Yes, our needy brothers may
judge us, but our Father is as loving as He is strict." It is a
long journey home from the foreign country, but he may
begin. We do not have enough clinical knowledge to say who
will return, how far, and why. We probably never will. This
is fundamentally the work of the Holy Spirit. "The wind
blows where it wills, and you hear the sound of it, but you
do not know whence it comes or whither it goes. . . ." Who
can explain the workings of God's Spirit?

Consider also the place of *preaching*. When the church
expands the place of involved liturgy at the expense of
preaching, she closes the door on any hope of breathing fresh
life into her children. The preacher alive with the urgent,
dynamic, unrestrained life of God cannot and will not be
hindered, and this is the mark of the greater preaching of our
time or any time. It is not the well-turned phrase or the
polished logic. It is the aliveness of God flowing freely over
the preacher's soul into the hearts and minds of expectant
people, leading them to see and feel the power of the cross
and resurrection for man here and now. The counselees who
say, "I wish I were dead," are deeply touched by this aliveness, and they can hear life calling to life. Many men who try

to evaluate the sermons of inspired preachers are not aware of this spark of unity with the heart of God; or sensing it, they do not find it in themselves through many hours of prayer over God's Word, and hope that by clever tricks they can generate it. No wonder laymen get neither help nor interference from the pulpit.

Preaching, of course, must be relevant. Questions that tickle our fancy may sound theological, but they only widen the gap between the real world and the world of the neurotic. The pastor stands before God to lift up the needs of the people. As ministers, we all do that in prayer, yes, but in the sermon persons come to experience their negative sets, their suspicions, their envy—and their never-destroyed longings to be themselves. The admonition of the church officer, "Don't tell us about man, Pastor, tell us about God," overlooks the fact that the Holy Spirit must prepare the heart of man to listen to the voice of God. Preaching is done well when the preacher loves and knows people, and each person feels God is speaking directly to him. It is a marvelous experience for the parishioner to hear the minister express certain facts about himself which he could never put into words. He cannot wait to rush to the door to pay him the highest compliment: "Marvelous sermon, Pastor! I understood most of what you were saying."

Preaching must also be paradoxical. How vital to preach the whole Word, as we read in II Timothy 4:2! Doing this avoids the one-sided legalism that retards the pharisaic mind.

In preaching the whole Word there seem to be contradictions. We say each man must bear his own burden. Next Sunday we say we will have to bear one another's burdens, and so fulfill the law of Christ. One Sunday we declare that we must separate ourselves from every hint of sin, for we are to be holy as He is holy. Next week we urge our people to follow

Christ to Capernaum, into the heart of throbbing life itself. Once we preach meekness and humility; the next time the loving of self and the gaining of confidence. Once we affirm the matchless joy of the Christian life; on another occasion we urge self-denial and the taking up of a cross.

Again and again we declare the sanctity of human passions, and the true worth of ambition, sex, desire for success, and the value of heated indignation when rightly directed. And then again we preach the power of self-sacrifice, stewardship beyond the tithe, and the losing of one's life for the sake of Christ and the gospel. These exhortations remind us that we are freed from the death of the Law's letter and are alive to the Spirit of life in Christ.

Preaching, above all, must be redemptive. What a thing to say! What else could it be? Well, it could be entirely philosophic, discussing God as if it were analyzing the GNP of the American economy. The resigned person could follow every point, but does he need scattered facts to preserve faith in a glass case? Not at all. He needs knowledge, but more than that he needs the Truth that lightens truth, Life that heals life, and the Way that leads back home. He needs the fullness of the Lord Jesus Christ in the depths of His being.

The pastor must be extremely careful that he does not capitalize on recessive trends of compliance and the desire of the neurotic to depend on him in the place of Christ. If attention is showered on the resigned person—or on any neurotic with deep trends of compliance—and then that attention is withdrawn, he will feel rejected and deeply hurt.

If the minister possesses pharisaic trends in himself, and if he cannot accept criticism or absorb negative feelings expressed by church members, then he has a problem which he must take to God and a deeply spiritual counselor. One of the glories of the true church is that both pastor and people stand dependent upon the one cross and its Christ.

The detached person is in need of squarely looking into the hell that has fired over into life, crucifying even God Himself. The cross enables him to face it without withdrawing into his shell. The means we employ to help the neurotic must have the cross and the resurrection at their center. The old gospel song has it right: "The Way of the Cross Leads Home." The same cross that opens wounds, heals them. There we can face guilt without being destroyed by anxiety. There we can afford to know ourselves as God knows us. In the crucified One we may recognize the uncertainty of our love for God, for others and for ourselves. We can do this when the depths of the unconscious are everlastingly assured of the certainty of His love for us.

We must carefully guard the happiness of so many who have been entrusted to us. Helping each to find confidence in life and in love is the chief expression of eternal life at work.

7

The Denouement

"DENOUEMENT" IS A LITERARY TERM FOR THE CONCLUDING action in stories and plays; the plot has been steadily brewing and suddenly comes to a boil. Webster defines it as: "1. The final revelation or occurrence which clarifies the nature and outcome of a plot. 2. The issue, outcome, or solution of a complex situation." The denouement in church life is a crisis in the power structure that shakes and divides the congregation as a growing earthquake crumbles the foundations of an otherwise solid building. Instead of regarding this trouble in the church as a family scandal that must at all costs be kept out of the papers, we ought to look hard and long at what it reveals.

The power structure of a church is the ruling coterie. It is the mutual-security arrangement of persons with the resources and desires to influence and govern the church. Unless the earthquake reaches into this power corps the tremors will fade. The anatomy of church life remains hidden unless objectively analyzed, or unless the denouement spews out into the open the volcanic forces of struggle and discontent precariously balanced and barely suppressed beneath the surface.

When trouble comes, little of redemption is brought to the layman. He is quietly asked, "For heaven's sake, can't you people out there settle that business?" Out of the question comes another indictment: "Isn't it the pastor's job to settle that? If he can't, he should leave the church, and our troubles will disappear."

What little redemption comes to the minister is in the form

of three types of books: 1) pure psychology, dealing with better techniques of counseling; 2) clever mechanical tricks for maintaining smooth administration; 3) a torrent of clichés advising the minister to be discreet with pretty girls, never to lose his temper, and to learn how to decline unnecessary engagements. If these had been followed like the Old Testament law no doubt trouble never would have flared out of hand and the "pastoral director" would have been more competent. No doubt.

The profession of medicine is not the use of all-purpose patent medicines for every disease. There is no medicine without diagnosis. If we pay the high price of trouble in so many churches, we ought to find out what this trouble is saying to us. What is the diagnosis? What is actually happening?

It is obvious that the following outline does not cover all the real factors in every church conflict in which disturbed persons play dominant roles. But it may provide a few helpful clues to the opening of a systematic approach to a whole new field of the psychology of Protestant church administration.

    I Threats to Self-Images
        A. Threats to the neurotic's idol
        B. Threats to the church's self-image; that is, to the church's idol
    II Conflict of Images
        A. Pastor-parishioner conflict
        B. Undermining the church's image
        C. Pastor's conflict with the denomination's self-image
        D. Conflict between the images of man and the image of God
    III Pastoral Ineffectiveness

A. Ineffectiveness with the neurotic personality
B. Ineffectiveness with the temporarily disturbed person
C. Ineffectiveness with frustrated and compensating persons
IV Conflict Takes Its Course
A. Common elements of the conflicts
B. A case in point
C. Intriguing questions on the nature of the conflict
V The Aftermath
VI Remedial Discussion

Let us peruse this outline to see what is meant by the terms used.

I Threats to Self-Images

A. Threats to the neurotic's idol. The neurotic person is very sensitive to being denied the satisfaction of public acceptance of the person he *must* be and assumes he is. The sensing by his subconscious that there is a cleavage between what he assumes he is and what others take him to be is experienced as guilt. He feels angry with himself for not measuring up to his self-image. He turns his hostility on the person considered responsible for revealing this cleavage.

For example, the resigned person may have strong trends of pharisaism and may rejoice at every fiery sermon against worldliness. This reinforces his position in his own eyes. He is above the hell-bound, sinful world. If anyone, however, makes it clear that this person has *specific* sins, and, let us say, goes so far as to name them, then terrible guilt is experienced. To say that the neurotic is enraged is putting it mildly. Whenever the critic is around, the disturbed person cannot rest. It is as if the critic is personally responsible for all the

·142·

uneasiness he has ever experienced. With him out of the way, life would be tranquil again. The critic's humiliation would only prove how right the pharisee really is. And the more rightness, the more safety—of that there must never be any doubt in his mind.

Another person may compartmentalize competing roles and images in his life. One image encourages conformity to the world, another to a church "in isolation" from the world. This becomes apparent, for example, when a respected member of the board of trustees works for a beer company and the pastor decides to campaign against the influence of the alcoholic beverage industry. Interpersonal conflicts are often the expression of intrapsychic conflicts (those within the person himself). If this board member lapses into anguish, he might feel inclined to take his suffering out on the pastor.

B. *Threats to the church's self-image.* Every church has a personality of its own. Every church has a ruling coterie, most of whom are on the official boards, some not. History, socio-economic levels, personality of the pastor, among many things, contribute to the church's self-image. The most important factor is the image the power structure needs to project.

A neurotic church is one that is separated from its true identity and is unable to undertake the mission dependent on that identity. It knows neither its true condition in the world nor in Christ, and lives in isolation to serve the ends of superiority and prestige. Its power structure centers around persons who are essentially frustrated in worldly ambition (and are compensating), or are neurotic.

The frustrated persons desire the whole church to satisfy their ambitions. One woman, aged seventy, said, "Our church contains the cream of the city, you know." I asked, "What do you mean, 'the *cream*'?" "Oh," she replied, "the people who count—the judges, lawyers, doctors, and those of us with outstanding professional service."

The church with a power structure built around one or more neurotic personalities is often not too concerned with what the world thinks. The "unenlightened" membership is the pyramid supporting the elite corps. But the whole neurotic struggle would be pointless without the subtle suspicions and competitions in the club within the church. They enjoy bewailing the indifference and pathetic spiritual condition of the church, and the club president says to his friends, "Without us—nothing!"

Wars, scientific discoveries and moon trips come and go, but in sick churches the power structure has one purpose: to continue forever the image they feel the local church should have of itself. It may be "the poor, struggling, inner-city church," or "the great historic church of Abe Lincoln," or "the church with the cream of the city," or "the only downtown church true to the historic old faith," but it must be made clear to the new pastor and new members that nothing can change. The new members are not much of a problem if the elite corps can be sure the new pastor will enlist them in dutifully subscribing to the glorified *status quo*.

II Conflict of Images

    A. Pastor-parishioner conflict. A pastor with a neurotic idol of his own does not see parishioners as persons in their own rights, but only as potential endorsements of the power and prestige of his idol. Competing idols may draw out spheres of influence, complement each other, or declare war.

A pastor with neurotic trends of masochism and morbid dependency will see himself as a suffering martyr. He will usually serve as the perfect match for a denominational or local church power structure gaining authoritarian momentum. All conflicts will be intrapsychic and the public will not see much trouble. Conflict, however, will be openly vicious if the neurotic trends of the pastor are a threat to destiny's club (that is, especially to its leaders).

We have, for example, observed closely several cases of a resigned and pharisaic pastor, with recessive trends of compliance, appealing to a pulpit-nominating committee because of his strict theology and fawning attitude. The power structure sees him as a humble and obedient servant who will enhance the image of a New Testament church that is true-blue to the faith once delivered. Naturally, it must be understood by all that it is true-blue because the elite corps is solidly on doctrinal course. Once the pastor is in the pulpit he decides to move into the driver's seat. Since those involved are absolutely correct theologically, there must be another arena of struggle such as choosing the furnishings or directing the building program. One senses that the keys of the kingdom unlock the treasury. One begins to hear that the "pastor lacks judgment, tact and common sense. He is a dictator." If he *can* be accused of harsh temper or indiscretion, so much the better. The negative set that feeds on the unending vindictiveness is based on the allegation that "he is unfit to be a minister."

   B. Undermining the church's image. The pastor has an image of himself, and, depending on the occasion, he may have a number of images of himself. This may also be said for each member. But the dominant image of the pastor may be in conflict with the image the church wishes to hold before itself.

For example, an evangelistic minister fresh out of seminary saw himself as a dynamic channel for the Word. His church in the center of the city appealed to itself as "the small, friendly, homogeneous, family church." The pastor saw this as a challenge. He envisioned it as a large, multiracial church for everyone. Leaders in the elite corps had grasped the church as the last barrier between themselves and a distant, misunderstanding world, and after four months they initiated a campaign to oust the pastor. It was unsuccessful. They had enlisted the support of the denomination to oust the former pastor and could not proceed with the same "charges" for the new man. As the reins of power began to be shared with unfamiliar hands, their hostility knew no bounds. The minister is still there.

C. Pastor's conflict with the denomination's self-image. See Vance Packard for some of the modern images of denominations. Each geographic or socio-economic area of the denomination will have an image slightly different than the one held by the whole.

A large, influential presbytery may picture itself as "strategic, rich, liberal, highly intellectual, containing key American cities." At a time when the moderator, stated clerk, executive and chairmen of two important committees consider the judicatory their private domain, a popular minister in a well-known church may be a fundamentalist who poses a direct threat to the elect corps. The power structure convinces other influential members of the presbytery that this man's church is giving the presbytery a black eye. He must go. It doesn't matter how he goes, or where—as long as he goes. Patiently they wait for their chance.

When this man finally makes a mistake, the campaign begins. Thereafter they collect *ex post facto* charges and recriminations. They continue jibing and attacking while they turn every anxious slip in speech or conduct, plus his every defensive effort, against him. When the case goes through the church courts they collect their "evidence," and assert that they have substantiated their charges from the beginning.

The evidence proves he is "lacking in judgment, intemperate, untruthful, too rigid in theology, and not scholarly and intellectual enough." Of course every minister may be guilty of these charges, and fifty per cent may be twice as guilty of any one as the man under attack. But no one has ever heard a churchman attack another through the church courts with the opening salvo, "Gentlemen, this man irritates me and I have finally found just reasons why he should irritate all of us."

   D. Conflict between the images of man and the image of God. "Now the Lord is the Spirit, and where the Spirit of the Lord is, there is freedom. And we all, with unveiled face, beholding the glory of the Lord, are being changed into his likeness from one degree of glory to another; for this comes from the Lord who is the Spirit."

When the Word of God is preached, the defensiveness of the sinner makes him initially hostile. The above passage tells us why. In the very course of a healthy church, a vital ministry for Christ comes into conflict with the dominion of evil.

The word for "change" in this Scripture means "transformed, transfigured, metamorphosized" (the biological process of radical change from one form to another). The word for "likeness" is *eikōn,* from which we get "icon," meaning "image."

We were created in God's image with God's gift of freedom in personality. That freedom was curtailed almost to the vanishing point by idolatry and sin.

Christ is truly Son of man and Son of God. He has emancipated us to the road of freedom. By His Spirit He changes our personalities into the images in which we were created. When our personalities are nurtured by the personality of Christ we become the persons God meant us to be, and we grow in freedom. Idolatry shackles. Christ liberates.

The liberating gospel is greeted with rebellion by the evil one. As the church herself becomes idolatrous she greets Christ's prophets with stones. As the church sinks deeper into idolatry she creates more conflict with every inward rush of the Spirit. Still, she abhors conflict because it is scandalous and antithetical to the image she wishes to hold before the world! If church and world slowly merge, the church turns and calls her own prophets "fanatics."

In growing into the likeness of Christ, the free system of Protestantism must first contend with itself. The church stands first to be known of God before she can make Him known to the world.

For example, art experts regularly face the problem of removing the paint from a canvas to reveal a superior masterpiece. Or they remove writing from a papyrus to uncover an earlier priceless manuscript. Just so, the Word of God is a detergent that irritates because it removes a surface image. It reveals the masterpiece of the cosmic Artist on the heart of every man He has ever made. It washes away that which is spurious and deceptive because it covers the divine workmanship (*poiēma*, Ephesians 2:11) on our hearts—which is the same epic poem of eternal love and holy power written into the heart of the universe (Romans 1:20).

The deceiver holds man in bondage by employing lies about the self as the antidote to anxiety. Evil rationalizes in its search to prove itself true and enduring. It is in eternal conflict with the truth of God. The conflicts that rage throughout New Testament history are not between religion and nonreligion, but between the power of the deceiver and the power of God.

The Christian is commited to this conflict. His Saviour made all things. His Lord wrestles with everything that is false and counterfeit in the universe. The Christian becomes an eternal life discerning the masks of time. He may live in the core of conflict and still have the peace of God in the core of his being. By most sincerely honoring God and himself he honors the true peace, purity and unity of the holy catholic church.

When the church opposes *per se* the very appearance of conflict, her leaders assume the church to be perfect. This assumption is, as we have seen, a form of idolatry. The call away from conflict is a call to cover God's image again and hide somewhere in the world. This call is madness. It is confusion gone to seed. No normal Christian could heed it because he is enjoying the normality of being one with God and with the heart of the universe. Deep down he senses that the call to "peace at any price" is a call to abnormality and the agony of dying. Either he finds courage to herald God's victory to the militant false faces of the world, or he cannot live with himself.

Fortunately, living with himself is precisely what Christ is enabling the healthy Christian to enjoy. For him to live is Christ, and physical death is gain. The possession of his soul is a joy he cannot afford to forfeit.

Before the church can endure the tension that results from witnessing to the world, she must be able to absorb the tension that results from witnessing to herself. No pastor should be forced to refrain from witnessing on the issues of alcoholism, racial segregation, economic justice and human freedom because he fears intimidation by a neurotic power structure. He does not wish to hear that a disturbed person in his church is telling his nervous denomination, "You see? We told you he is a troublemaker!" If he cannot minister to the world because he cannot minister to his church, then fear reigns. A shudder goes through the ranks: "Put on a mask because your brother might be an enemy." But what mask? How hide? From whom?

III Pastoral Ineffectiveness

A. Ineffectiveness with the neurotic personality. In the Protestant church the pastor does not officiate from the distance of a priest. He ministers immersed in the very life-stuff of his people. In this he is one with Christ. He leads the church, and yet he throws himself into the secret heart of his people. He eats, talks, mingles, counsels, weeps, laughs and prays with them. They make the maximum demands on his spirit. They empty out his mind, wring out his heart for more comfort, and hope for a sign from him when hope flickers.

They know he isn't God. They remind themselves that "You ministers are human, like everybody else." But when God doesn't come through as they had hoped, they are apt to wonder why the pastor didn't have a bit more influence with heaven. This is natural.

The pastor frustrates them further by reminding them of their sins. Said one lay preacher to men noted for their piety, "You stiff-necked people, uncircumcised in heart and ears, you always resist the Holy Spirit. As your fathers did, so do you. Which of the prophets did not your fathers persecute?"

Absorbing this hostility, and reflecting in turn the cleansing forgiveness of God, is the pastor's golden opportunity to focus the power of the cross for his people. While he lives with them on the growing edges of their souls he must demonstrate spiritual leadership and competence to aid the Holy Spirit in lifting them God-ward. By his own life he encourages them to enforce words of testimony with lives of grace.

The pastor is a human being beset with the struggles and temptations of all men. His dare to accept the leadership in ministry is possible only by the Spirit's call and the promise of Christ's power. Preaching will do miracles, not because he is miraculous, but because its subject is the Word of God. The pastor, then, needs the church as much as the church needs him. He requires their grace and prayers as much as they look to his certain leadership.

The neurotic personality does not see the pastor in this light. We have explained why in previous chapters. Suffice it here to say that he is hypnotized by the pastor's authority and status. He feels that he is a power to be reckoned with, a competition to be curtailed, an authority to be wooed, and a giant to be cut down to size. He continually goes out of his way to prove that the pastor is an ordinary fellow who makes mistakes, like everyone else.

Because the neurotic personality to some extent desires to be dependent on great power (satellization), and still be the all-sufficient source of all-power himself, he is naturally confused by the minister's role. He longs for the pastor to be an omniscient leader without interfering, a perfect father without disciplining, and a replica of Christ without emotion. He wants him to take responsibility for the neurotic's life without making recommendations contrary to his own. He wishes him, in short, to cure his hell by reconciling his irreconcilable needs.

Partially this explains why the neurotic is wildly enthused about the coming of the new minister and "what he is going to do for our church." By the third month or sooner, he is convinced the minister is a tragic disappointment.

It is clear that when the pastor antagonizes the neurotic person, or possesses neurotic trends in conflict with his, he will bear the brunt of vindictiveness. Actually, this vindictiveness is partially fed by disappointment. Deep down and only vaguely, the neurotic hopes for some sort of salvation, some way out of conflicting emotions. He needs help, though he has no idea how or from where it will come. He expects the pastor to do wonders. If his hopes are met with fumbling and bumbling, with hasty, ineffectual counseling, with outright rejection, or with harsh advice, he is angry with himself for contravening his own defenses and becoming, to some degree, overly dependent. He feels humiliated that he did not believe his own subconscious philosophy that "most people cannot be fully trusted." Any self-hate experienced will soon be turned on the pastor.

The neurotic pastor is in the same dilemma. He hopes the new church will be his salvation. He begins like a rocket to the outer reaches of glory. When his unrealistic hopes are dashed to the ground, all his troubles become "their fault."

Already one denomination is setting up counseling and therapy centers, staffed by volunteers, in key churches throughout the state. The time may come when disturbed persons may benefit by long-term therapy at minimal cost. At present, however, pastors must deal with the disturbed person where he is, before he consciously recognizes any need for help. An effective ministry to the neurotic requires training and competence, and this is in addition to the other specialized preparation which ministers come to think of as absolutely essential.

 B. *Ineffectiveness with the temporarily disturbed person.* Quite often one wonders how a slight disturbance by isolated neurotic vindictiveness can suddenly envelop a whole church in flames. This is because key persons suddenly sympathize with the complaints of the neurotic. They may have held incipient resentment that the pastor did not help them in their time of dire need. Very likely he was not aware of their needs.

Mrs. L. was the church secretary and a church member. She was in the process of getting a divorce. One evening her husband was killed in an automobile accident. Several months later the pastor assumed she was feeling well. She never mentioned her husband's death. She went about her church activities as usual. And it wasn't as if the family was broken up by the death, because Mrs. L. once confided she didn't love her husband and she was prepared to live without him.

When the minister saw Mrs. L., everything was business. The church had work to do and he breathed a sigh of relief that Mr. L.'s death did not slow down the vital machinery of the Kingdom. His discussions always centered around letters and stencils, and he once remarked that she had won a fine spiritual victory.

Actually, Mrs. L. was hiding from grief. She felt intensely guilty when her husband died, and she was not reaching into the depths to face her true condition with God. Later, when trouble came to the church, the pastor was shocked to learn that Mrs. L. agreed he was "just not a good minister people could go to in time of need."

Here was a case in which trouble flared even when the pastor considered the smooth working of the machinery as his chief goal. The theater remained open for business while one of the stars was dying before the director's eyes.

C. Ineffectiveness with frustrated and compensating persons. When church members hold to the minister as the one chiefly responsible for the success (whatever that may mean) or failure of the church, the pastor himself may become party to a conspiracy of hero-worship. In such cases he prizes highly the members who labor assiduously with heavy responsibility. They contribute to his success, but he may be neglecting their deepest spiritual needs. This is particularly true where persons unsatisfied in work, or living in the deflated self-evaluation of retirement, look to the church as their nexus of regained pride and status. The more frustrated they feel elsewhere, the more the church becomes the road back to feeling wanted or even greatly admired. Some official board members lean back and imagine themselves as chairmen once again of the board of the corporation. The house of God is now their own private possession. There is nothing they wouldn't do for it, provided they are heard with respect and remain on the board of directors.

These men are often the most determined to put the same premium on other-directed smiling conformity in church that they did in business. In their days the organization polished culture's men and fitted them into the economic machine as well-oiled cogs. When the church spins silently on deadcenter, like a top, they are grateful they've never lost their old touch. The oily young cogs filling the pews these days should appreciate the deft and dapper touch of the old machine foremen.

This does not mean these men have neurotic trends, although some crisis at work or in retirement may have made them victims of a situational neurosis. If the pastor makes a "deal" with them, whereby they leave him alone, provide a good salary, and take care of the manse, while he in turn does not interfere with them, then he is refusing to minister to their souls. Later they may resent a new minister as an unwanted interference. His coming engenders anxiety, and they may be suspicious that his leadership could upset the congregation's uniform and spiritless response to Madison Avenue programs—which is too likely to be called the "unity of the church."

These people often rebel against specific and forceful

preaching of justification by faith. They have never stopped playing to the balcony. They are essentially pragmatic and dearly love ways and means that work. As board members they see their jobs as mass-producing clever keys to unlock heaven's gates. They're not sure what to do with the idea that heaven was opened by the blood of the Lamb. While they're tinkering with the idea, they still believe firmly in justification by works.

A dynamic, imaginative pastor will find his initial efforts going down the drain if every move isn't baptized with patience. If enough of these people are in the power structure with a neurotic leader, he may find his efforts going there anyway.

IV. Conflict Takes Its Course

A. Common elements of the conflicts. The leader in the power structure is usually a respected, spiritual and capable Christian man. Both pastor and people look to him. But this position isn't always held by such a person. The lust for power in some form on the part of the neurotic personality makes him a pivotal force in many power structures. Rarely is he content to sit on the sidelines unseen.

The expansive-vindictive personality at the center of the power corps views the whole structure in terms of the safety of his own position. When a negative set evolves and he informs his associates that the target is the pastor, he is, in a sense, greatly relieved. All elements of the situation are clarified and the goal is clear: remove the minister.

The neurotic person knows that at first he cannot take the lead in pressing for the minister's removal, or for the ouster of any enemy in church. Thoroughly convinced of the rightness of his position, he waits and patiently collects scraps of information that he hopes to use later. Every chance remark about the minister is dutifully recorded on paper or mentally.

Unobtrusively, at first, he feeds negative conversations. Like Absalom, he heartily agrees with everyone who has a complaint about anything. Bishop Gerald Kennedy has given us "A Handy Guide to Parish Phrases" in *The Episcopalian:*

"He is not a spiritual preacher" means "His message is too relevant."

"He brings politics into the pulpit" means "I do not agree with him."

"He speaks out with courage" means "I agree with him."

"He is pink" means "He dares to criticize the *status quo.*"

"His attitude will hurt church finances" means "I will cut my subscription from 50 cents a week to 25 cents."

"He is sowing dissension" means "Some people are waking up."

"He must consider his position" means "I want an emasculated citizen in the pulpit."

"He lacks judgment" means "He takes Jesus seriously."

"He neglects the substantial members" means "The church is beginning to move."

"He plays up to the new members" means "He is bypassing the roadblocks we set up."

"He upsets my faith" means "My prejudices are taking a beating."

"The whole church is upset" means "I am causing all the trouble I can."

The person with a vested interest in pushing this conflict in church life from stage to stage has no trouble in believing his own pessimism. He looks everywhere and sees a terrible situation developing. The cat is out of the bag when he confides to close friends, "There is a feeling of restlessness in our church now, that I haven't detected for years." And no doubt it is to his interest that everyone feels as restless as he does.

Thereafter, the strategy of the negative set is quite simple and almost universal. The neurotic personality feeds the flames generously while absolving himself of any responsibility for the fire. He sees to it that matters stay in a state of confusion. He weeps to officers and to the denomination, "This man must go, for the good of the church. We must not think in terms of personalities. It is the peace and unity of Christ's Kingdom that must be uppermost in our hearts." This form of blackmail means, "There will be no peace until the minister leaves. My friends and I will see to that."

The whole movement to triumph over the pastor would die of exhaustion if it were not for the vindictiveness of the key expansive-vindictive leaders, usually not more than two or three—often just one. One or two women set up headquarters and run them like party offices in a national election. They write letters and use the phone half the day and most of the evening.

The entire church buzzes with the constant drone of gossip. Each new revelation of some evil the pastor has done helps keep The Issue alive. All conversations get around to The Issue. Each new caucus receives reports from party leaders while the campaign feeds on itself. After an hour of bringing themselves to a white-heat hostility, a party caucus is supercharged with emotion which they hope to convey to denominational officers. The rest of the church is surprised at the fire and urgency of their cause, and shrug their shoulders in dismay. They do not observe the minister growing horns, but alas! where there's smoke, there's fire—somewhere.

One sometimes wonders how allegedly Christian people can suddenly find themselves becoming part of a velvet Mafia in church. The affair first takes on the aspects of a Lilliputian comic opera on a soapbox. Later it becomes apparent that

·157·

enlistment in a hate program has brought significance and recognition to some people for the first time in many long years. The Issue turns into The Cause, from which there is no retreat.

Pastors in such situations almost always continue living by the Sermon on the Mount, assuming this vindictiveness will sooner or later run out of steam. After a particularly blessed worship service the pastor gives thanks to God that now he has heard the last of this maelstrom. Several leaders of the dissident minority, however, consider this very clever strategy. The minister's spiritual front only confirms their judgment that he is a hypocrite, *par excellence*, preying on the innocent. No sooner is the benediction pronounced than they fly about like lobbyists at a Washington hearing, collaring stray votes and potential recruits.

The leader of the minority resigns or threatens to resign from the church or official board. The neurotic with any trends of expansiveness, we must remind ourselves, is not putting up a big front in his own eyes. In his conscious mind he is honestly convinced that he *is* his defensive facade, and that his claims are entirely justified. He does not honestly see how the church could operate without him, and he assumes that his threat to resign will be an earthquake to bring everyone to his senses. He further assumes that the minister will fall into the trap, accept his resignation, and the horrified congregation will see the minister for what he is. He stays away for several weeks to give everyone a taste of the danger.

If the pastor has vindictive aspects to his own personality, The Issue becomes inflamed. When the minister and his friends initiate a counter-campaign, the dissident leader views it as an outrageous offensive. His philosophy is, "I am privileged to do what I wish, and others are privileged only to agree with the rightness of my position." The minister's at-

·158·

tempts to defend himself are interpreted as justification for the neurotic's aggression.

Pious phrases and superficial attempts to patch up any differences are worse than useless. The dissident leaders are not dealing with people or situations, but with their own anxiety. They are dumbstruck if the church progresses in their short absence, if others can claim the minister is helping them, if lightning does not strike when they threaten to resign, and if new members are assuming their former responsibilities. They could never live with themselves in the church or out of it if they were to withdraw and tacitly admit defeat. They see no alternative but to press the attack, tighten their defenses, and justify themselves in the eyes of the world. That is why, in the denouement, when the pastor is sure God will straighten matters out, matters get worse.

After one or two years of conflict, the neurotic personality is thoroughly convinced that anything goes. He confides to associates that he has been "much in prayer" about The Issue, and he must protect the church. This includes five steps:

1) Accuse the pastor of lying. The minister is talking all the time, while the dissident minority is listening. Months later they will ask him what he said and will have witnesses to prove he said something different. In conversations with individuals, it is their word against his.

2) Meet with sympathetic denominational representatives. While the attendance and offerings are increasing, the word is passed that the congregation is driven to distraction and no one is giving regularly and few are attending. On the one hand, the complaint is made that strange lower-class persons are now filling the pews and, on the other, that none but the most loyal old members now attend services.

One must add that if the situation continues, it is too diffi cult for progress to be made. Dr. Richard K. Morton reminds us: "In my own experience there have been literally scores of people turned from the organized churches—even while loving their Lord and believing deeply in the Christian faith—because of the hypocrisy, the barrage of criticism, and the attitude of contention and strife on the part of members. Many have grown disgusted with the suspicion, prejudices, rivalries, and narrow policies in many of these churches, and have felt that there is nothing which they can gain by staying with them. . . . We cannot attribute all this to loss of faith or poor witness or lack of consecration. A pastor reasonably gets tired of being harried and pressured to do what he cannot possibly do—and then be criticized unthinkingly by those who have no regard for the truth, for personal feelings or for the cause of the Church." Eventually the denomination is impressed with the fact that there is unrest in the church and many persons are tired of it.

3) Look into the minister's past. The dissident group cannot tolerate the suspicion that anything is wrong with them. If they are always the ones to complain, it is because of their superior insight and spirituality. Their problems on this score could be solved if it were advertised that the minister also had trouble in former churches. They investigate.

4) Prevent salary increases. It is stated that any increase in salary would further upset the church. The manse roof may be caving in. Repairs might be mistaken as a peace token by some, so none are undertaken.

5) Resort to outright fear. We had a case in a New England presbytery in which the manse was actually bombed by a successful banker who was unsuccessful after several years of feuding with the pastor.

It is not uncommon for the pastor to receive telephoned threats, to be denounced in abusive language, and to receive poison-pen letters. Ministers usually leave when they feel that this is more than their families can endure.

   B. A case in point.

 ▣ ▣ ▣

Pastor X held a thriving and deeply spiritual pastorate for nearly a decade and left it with two thousand members. In July 1960, he moved to a church with fifteen hundred members in another state. The church held a definite image in the community for forty years and advertised itself in the newspapers as "The church of which Dr. _____ _____ was the minister." It was completely dedicated to the past. On special occasions, such as the annual meeting, its time was spent delving into or hearing a report on the life and works of the famous minister.

For thirty-eight years Pastor X's predecessor had had a working agreement with the power structure and interfered not at all in their operations. In 1942 he went through the secular courts to get himself adopted to inherit a woman's fortune, while his own mother was still living. The power structure adjusted their morality to condone this.

In 1922 the church had gone through the secular courts and the legislature of the state to set up an independent board of trustees (in addition to the regular board) to handle an endowment fund. This board never reported to the congregation. It was self-perpetuating. It was made up mostly of men from the other boards.

In 1955 the pivotal personality of the power structure, a former president of a giant corporation, Mr. D., set up a Challenge Fund. The power structure worshiped Mr. D., who gave a great deal to benevolences and was considered a kind and generous man. No officers, however, expected to remain on the board if they crossed him. The structure around Mr. D. was stable. The chief governing body, the session, nominated members whose terms had expired, and the congregation dutifully re-elected them.

Mr. D. was the man who paid all debts not covered by the offerings. His wife was called Dorothy, and the church was affectionately known in the community as "St. Dorothy's." The Challenge Fund matched fifty cents of Mr. D.'s money for every dollar given by the congregation toward a new building program. Mr. D. chose the architect and decided on the plans. In 1959 he died. His will set up a "Secret Fund," to be administered by two anonymous trustees, for the benefit of the church. Although the two men were members of the other boards, this "Secret Fund" was known by the congregation.

The power structure included the treasurer who was also treasurer of presbytery and synod. He succeeded in getting synod to set up its own independent endowment fund.

Other members of this power structure were relatives, business associates, and friends of many years. Old retired men on the boards agreed *in toto* with their directions, knowing that they were elected through the influence of these other persons. Their lives, hobbies and work were the church.

After Mr. D.'s death the reins of pivotal power passed into the hands of Mr. L. J., a former bandleader, now an attorney, who had been groomed for the position by Mr. D.

When Pastor X arrived on the field he delved into the secret funds and unconstitutional procedures. He noted that the church had no budget, gave no sound financial report to the corporation, and conducted fifteen-minute session meetings followed by an evening of gay fellowship.

Pastor X added choirs, encouraged the congregation to sing three hymns in the services of worship, instituted classes in Calvinism, the Bible and Communism. He preached the Word in love, began an evangelistic program, and made the liturgy a more striking vehicle of the incarnation, death and resurrection.

One of the board members drew out Pastor X concerning his plans and his opinions of the secret funds. Pastor X made the remark in his conversation that some of the procedures were dishonest. The member ran back to the power structure and told all.

After a morning evangelistic sermon in which the pastor announced that any and all persons in the community were to be welcomed into the church, key persons in the power structure met and announced to each other, "This man must go." Said Mr. L. J., "We realized within a month or two after Dr. _____ was here that he wasn't going to do—not at all!"

The negative set went into action. The congregation was fed the "news" that the pastor did not pay his bills, wasn't to be trusted with women, had an illegitimate son, was not tactful, and that he insulted respected officials by calling them "dishonest." The "illegitimate son" business was an outright lie, the allegations concerning women were lies, and the rest were almost total distortions. The pastor did, however, say some of the officials were dishonest.

When new members began to take hold and compete with the old power structure, the dissident minority met frequently and became more aggressive. They hired detectives to trace the pastor's former ministry, and to follow him in his present field.

Pastor X did not feel he could go to another minister in his presbytery, and certainly not to its officials. There was no one to talk to, to confide in, nothing but a vast and somber sea of loneliness. He finally opened his heart to an Episcopal bishop.

The presbytery's ministerial relations committee was called in. This committee did what all similar committees do: it recognized that the peace of the church was marred—with regret, of course. The overwhelming majority of the church was strongly in favor of the pastor, but the peace was shattered. No doubt about it.

The power structure and denominational officials offered the pastor some ripe plums if he would move. They did not say where to—just move. When he remained, an administrative commission was appointed. This commission received a letter from the power structure saying that if Pastor X would leave, ten members of their group would resign.

The commission had neither the time, inclination, nor resources to study the interpersonal dynamics of this ill church. It ordered the minister and ten elders to resign, but the minister was to leave the church and the elders were to resign from the official board while remaining in the church. Pastor X did not have a call to another church when his time ran out and he and his wife moved back to their former state. He lived on the year's advance salary given by the church.

The ten elders who were ordered to resign from the session remained in their other responsibilities in the church. Those who were members of the secret board and secret funds continued as usual.

Pastor X was finally called by an eastern presbytery to act as interim pastor of a church whose minister and session were ordered to resign by an administrative commission.

◧ ◧ ◧

C. Intriguing questions on the nature of the conflict.
1) Do theological differences play a major part? Theological differences are usually not the actual underlying factors. Many conservative pastors have been able to go into extremely liberal churches and patiently build an effective ministry for Christ. There is likely to be more disturbance if a very conservative church becomes fearful that a liberal pastor is attempting to change their thinking. Capable men have

successfully aided negative and pharisaic churches "in isolation."

The essential factors are the threats to, and conflicts of, images. An unconverted, extremely liberal, expansive-vindictive personality in a pivotal position may even be quite taken up with Biblical preaching. When, however, Christ speaks to him about the cleavage between his profession and defensive facade, anything can happen. The anxiety generated by the Holy Spirit (the image of God versus the images of man) will make him sensitive to the slightest tinge of insult or competition. Once a negative set evolves, the neurotic personality sees constructive Biblical preaching as a personal attack on him from the protection of the pulpit.

The morbidly dependent person with liberal doctrinal views may feel that judgment, holiness and hell portray a vindictive God believed in by a rejecting minister. If the pastor rides these doctrines as a hobby horse to work out his own personal conflicts, this person will sense it and feel alienated.

Generally, the neurotic person is more concerned about the minister's attitude toward him as a person than about his doctrinal position. He differs from other members however, in that when a negative set reveals itself the doctrinal issues become quite useful. He can refer to the prevailing denominational philosophy to indict a conservative pastor, and can refer to the historic confessions to condemn a liberal minister.

2) What about the many neutral persons in a church conflict? Neutral persons are those who do not take a stand against the pastor for the first six months. Great pressure is brought to bear on them by the power structure and their friends. When a neutral does not bend to their thinking it is made crystal clear that when the minister goes, the security of all on the wrong side of the fence will be in jeopardy. The neutrals may then compromise their consciences. They have

known the minister for a year or so. They have known their friends for years. Some day the minister will leave and they will have to go back to their friends.

Vindictive persons assume their enemies are vindictive. All they can say to the neutrals is, "Keep an eye on him and you will see what we mean." The leaders of the power structure become like members of the Communist Party around the world, capitalizing on every disorder and irritation they find, whether or not it has anything to do with their program. A negative approach to life breeds in discontent and feeds it.

The neutrals have been profiting from the pastor's work. Persons are growing in Christ. They show their affection in many quiet ways and invite him to their homes for meals. They become heartsick over the acrimony and confusion. The bitterness wears many of them down to superficial participation in church life. Some see what the power structure is doing and support the minister vociferously. Some are torn between the demands of their friends and loyalty to the minister. When the minister sees that loyalty to Christ ought to be the first concern of every believer, he is torn between loyalty to the One who called him to the church and to the members who look to him to cure the sick church, and loyalty to wife and children. If no one comes to his aid, and to the aid of the church, he may no longer be able to watch disappointment and bitterness capture the hearts of many of the Lord's own. He keenly feels his wife's suffering.

3) What about the neurotic personality who is not in the power structure? An expansive-vindictive personality, for example, may or may not be on one of the boards. If not, and if he is not a member of long standing with considerable influence, his resentment has a nil effect. He may encourage others to side with him, but they will refuse. He will be heard to say, "The men on that board are a group of rubber

stamps for the minister." This may be perfectly true, but if the pastor is serving the power structure, they will ignore opposition until it dies. If it persists, they will probably discipline the offender.

4) To what degree are these tensions and conflicts responsible for ministers' nervous breakdowns? Those recovering from so-called nervous breakdowns alarm us by commenting, "Oh, I guess I've just been working too hard." Did they have extensive counseling in depth? Has God revealed more of Himself to them? Has He revealed more of themselves to their own eyes? Will they inflame similar conflicts elsewhere? Are they gaining or losing confidence in themselves? In people?

In this field much work in testing and clinical investigation is sorely needed. There are too many guesses and not enough concrete objective deduction and analysis. It is hoped that when our major denominations install area pastors thoroughly trained in clinical psychology they will meet for seminars and conferences to pool their information and thus eliminate futile hit-and-miss attempts to understand and help deteriorating ministers.

The Cleveland Clinic contains a barnful of test data on Episcopal preministerial students. There is no follow-up testing years later in the pastorate. What, if any, is the relationship between breakdown and the high tendency toward femininity in students, noted by the psychologists? Taking into account the whole array of pressures on the minister, against the background of our culture and its demand for conformity, have we failed to note clues in this data to future breakdowns? Only hard work and objective thinking will help us find the answers.

V The Aftermath

The denouement for an individual may be an identity crisis used by God to reveal human defense and sinfulness.

The denouement for a church likewise reveals true conditions. If prompt redemptive measures are brought to bear, Christ may be born in the travail of conflict. There is no need for it to proceed to destructive stages. When the first symptoms reveal conflict, there is urgent opportunity. All such crises, whether individual or congregational, are the price we pay to see ourselves and do something about it.

When a committee announces, "Once these conflicts get going you cannot stop them, so it is better to leave now," it pays a high tribute to impotence. This grave pronouncement is the veneer or superficiality. The pastor and his flock are not a barricaded island. They are the church. They may need help together. If the whole church cannot bring redemption and judgment to one of its parts, then the whole organism is sicker than we know.

What shall we say when the same committee requests the minister to pull up roots and forsake his ministry, demands that the Holy Spirit call him immediately to another charge and take his family to another city? Authority demands responsibility, and responsibility requires loving service. If executives and committees cannot take the time for responsibility, they should not be granted the authority. Many of them are busy pastors themselves, but aggravating the condition by attempting to throw it out the window is enough to make the church cynical of herself.

Ministers are offered plums and promised large churches if they will quietly disappear. When they do, they never hear from the committee, never receive ministry, know little of love's gracious inclusiveness.

Meanwhile, the testimony of the church is finished for one or two decades. The disgruntled neurotic personalities are like Humpty Dumpties who resign some of their major responsibilities after their mighty fall, and they begin a desperate campaign to mend broken fences and defenses. They are bewildered that happiness does not fly into their souls like a bird after the inglorious triumph over their target. They are annoyed with those who did not side with them from the beginning. They fear that perhaps they revealed a wrong side of themselves to too many people. The old days are gone forever.

The truth is that no one is satisfied, and could not be, in the very nature of a condition that sent down roots before the denouement. There is no easy cure for a severe illness, even though shooting the patient in hysterical despair might be said to terminate it for good. When a member of Christ's one Body is ill, whether church or individual, it is the problem of each of us and we must work where we are to bring God's healing. If the church has no cure for herself, what does she offer the world?

VI Remedial Discussion

If you are a layman in a church where these tensions are growing, there is much you can do. Let us list a constructive course:

1) Co-operate with the Lord in making the denouement a means of salvation. To do this you will need to purify your heart with a daily Bible reading. Especially apply Proverbs 19-22 to your own condition.

2) Pray daily that God might assist pastor and people to think clearly, decide with courage and act with patience. Pray that in all things the Holy Spirit might do His holy work in the people's hearts.

3) Disengage yourself from any crusading loyalties. In one situation a woman remarked, "I'm so confused. I don't know which side to be on." The conviction that one must take

sides is utterly childish. The church is not a private club. Your friendship with Christ rules all other friendships. Stop feeling that you are a crusader, that you must ride out and inflame tensions. You have one business in the church: to be obedient to God.

4) Be redemptive with all persons. Under no circumstances carry gossip. Not only are talebearing and slander considered vile sins in the New Testament, but their presence in your life inhibits any redemptive action whatever on your part. You only withdraw from the solution and become a major part of the problem.

5) Be a trusted friend. The term, in psychotherapy, has special meaning. It signifies the usefulness of any lay person in enabling another to reveal and deal constructively with turbulent emotions. This is accomplished by patient and creative listening, while refraining from judgments and advice.

A trusted friend does not ask questions. He carefully follows what the other person is saying. He refrains from arguments and persuasiveness. When he hears something in trusted friendship he repeats it to no one, and certainly to no member of his family.

6) Use a little self-control. Others may derive a certain satisfaction in yielding to the mass tension or even to the spirit of the lynch mob, but not you. When you go to church, forget yourself. Discipline yourself to pray, meditate and receive benefit from the sermon. If some of your friends give the appearance of aged prophets weighted down with the burden of The Issue, you can set an example of poise and good will. "Blessed are the peacemakers, for they shall be called sons of God."

7) Use your responsibility with intelligence. Some time you may have to vote at a congregational meeting or speak to a

denominational representative. Speak what you know and feel, wisely and courteously, betraying no confidences.

If you are a Protestant you are part of a democratic church and cannot avoid your responsibilities. Do not succumb to implied threats or to fear of rejection. Respect your brothers in Christ.

8) Honor your minister. Remember that your pastor could not have gone through seminary, been examined by his denomination, done the work of ministry in former churches, and served the Lord from morning to night on a small salary if he were an unscrupulous person. When you see his faults you have the opportunity to exercise the grace you have been hearing about in your faith for years. His ministry is not predicated upon perfection any more than yours. Charges against him are a deadly serious business. Those making them must substantiate them through the judicial processes of the church, not by destructive gossip. Outside of three ministerial failures that have come to our attention in ten years, the gossip of church members has caused more lasting harm than any error in judgment by the pastor of those churches.

If your denomination has a minister who serves as bishop or spiritual advisor to your own pastor (area pastor is the name we are giving this spiritual advisor or counselor), by all means open your heart to him if he wishes to speak with you. Your pastor may have personality habits that hinder his work. He may have failed to do his best in ministering to you. Tell the area pastor how you feel and he will hold your statements in absolute confidence. His dealings with your pastor will be entirely redemptive, and your pastor will prove more capable through your assistance.

If your denomination has no such full-time counselor, do not under any circumstances tell your story to another pastor. The only time your minister can reasonably profit is when you speak to a denominational representative officially designated to assist pastor and church, and only when this official takes the time to calmly and patiently counsel with you in private. Telling your story as gossip to other church members, or to persons outside the church, constitutes sufficient grounds for censure, and if continued, for church discipline either by the official board or your denomination. Occasionally, at open meetings sponsored by the denomination's representatives, members of the dissident minority spew out any gossip and make any unsubstantiated charge against the pastor that comes to mind. This sort of thing is too unspeakably disgraceful to merit intelligent discussion.

If your pastor has failed you or irritated you, do not ignore your feelings. Speak directly to him. Never be sorry you opened your heart to him. If he has a growing soul he will be indebted to you. If your problem concerns such personal habits as slurring over words or distracting pulpit mannerisms, go to the official board member you know best and deeply respect. He will be glad to help his minister. Some people are well-acquainted with the minister's wife, and they should feel free to speak to her. When no one else will tell the pastor the facts, his wife can carry the ball. They may be in love, but pastors long ago learned not to ask their wives, "Who said that?"

There are times when a pastor runs deeply against your grain. Others work with him cordially and you dislike him more and more. You don't really understand why, you have no intention of permitting him to counsel you, and you refuse to discuss it with the area pastor. You suspect he is somehow in conflict with a self-image, or threatens you in some way. What to do?

In this case you must beware above all else of seeking popular confirmation of your self-image and your status. Pray for a cool head and a warm heart. You may decide that your only sensible course is to attend another church. There is not one rule in the course of human affairs which states that all pastors will be effective with all persons. Think of the church as the holy catholic church. Worship God elsewhere, and pray for guidance in your search for the deepest level of your being. The time will surely come when you can return to your church as a better person. Or God may lead you to be a stronger disciple where you have gone. Remember that the church does not belong to you. It belongs to the Lord Jesus.

These rules of church etiquette are simple expressions of the elementary kindness Paul speaks of in I Corinthians 13. The world may have stopped looking to us for miracles, but it can still rely on us, we feel sure, for the courtesy marking any decent man.

And what of the ministers who find themselves in these situations? Ministers who have been used mightily of God in churches large and small shared this advice: First, begin a program of visitation and small group discussions before changing any part of the existing order. Know your people well. Work patiently. Be grateful for those who respond to God, and work slowly and prayerfully with those who are waiting. From start to finish, depend on God and free yourself from the tyranny of self-doubt and self-abnegation.

In prayer and daily Bible study, live close to Christ. Never stop growing. Keep these near your desk: *The Growing Minister,* by Andrew Blackwood (Abingdon Press); *The Christian Shepherd,* by Seward Hiltner, and his *Preface to Pastoral Theology* (Abingdon Press); *Disorders of the Emotional and Spiritual Life,* by W. L. Northridge (Channel Press). Read widely on counseling, consulting *Pastoral Work and Personal Counseling,* by Russell L. Dicks (The Macmillan Company); *Psychology of Counseling,* by Clyde Narramore (Zondervan Publishing House); and *The Art of Counseling,* by Rollo May (Abingdon Press).

Prepare for a long pastorate. Be thoroughly acquainted with your denominational constitution and the judicial procedures for protecting a man's name and ministry. In a busy schedule take the time to plan your leadership. Use *Pastoral Leadership* by Andrew Blackwood (Abingdon Press), and remember his words: "Let every pastor and his associates understand that more is done, or lost by neglect of doing, on a new member's churchmanship in the first three years of his affiliation than in all his years of discipline afterwards."

Understand how to prepare the ground for conversion so that you do not employ evangelism as a means of subjugating persons. Read *The Psychology of Christian Conversion,* by Robert O. Ferm (Fleming H. Revell Company).

Meet regularly with other ministers in a sharing of minds and souls. Talk from time to time with an area pastor. Keep open the lines of communication with wife, church officials and members. When you are criticized, evaluate the criticism; if it contains a grain of truth, act on it. See whether you are bulldozing through your church, pushing, selling and talking every inch of the way. Instead, draw your people out so that they feel free to express themselves. Everyone gets angry and disappointed, but when the minister won't stand still long enough to listen and understand, these people are going to get angrier.

The moment you see symptoms of trouble getting beyond you, call the area pastor. You are too close to the situation to see it clearly. Do not talk with members to lessen your anxiety, especially when some are tempted to mangle your statements in gossip. And think of what you are saying to your wife. Is she resentful that home life is becoming the occasion for caustic free association on The Issue?

Flush out of your heart any vindictiveness. Be watchful that in the pulpit you minister to all the people. It may be necessary to slow down the entire program, and this is heart-breaking. Be careful in word and deed never to retaliate.

If the immediate denomination has a power structure which is inept, authoritarian, and calloused, patiently wait upon the Lord. Think carefully. Respect your high calling by the Spirit. You cannot act with omniscience, but only on the light you have. Some men have walked with God through the storm and now have happy and prospering churches. Others and their families could not tolerate their own anxiety.

Some men made a beginning and decided it was best to leave after a year or two, praying that another could build on their foundation work. A few who were forced to leave waited several months before accepting a new charge in order to work with a spiritual therapist in studying their self-images and how the self-images of the power structure were threatened.

Who is to say what you should do and what is right? If after prayer and discussion with the area pastor you have done as much as you can, move on. While you are waiting to move, pray for the church. Read the gospels through slowly, then the Acts. See how the Word of God goes about. In some places men run out to greet it and hungrily reach for every syllable. Others merely hear. Some turn away. A few become violently angry, pick up stones and begin throwing them at the prophet. Sometimes the prophet moves on. He may be stoned and begin again. He may be stoned to death. Or crucified. So it was with Christ. And so with some who take up their crosses.

It must become the task of the whole church to train her leaders to be more adept in ministry to the neurotic personality. Some shepherds have splendid powers of preaching and imaginative leadership. With assistance they can gain victory over neurotic trends in themselves and become a marvelous source of inspiration to Christ's church.

Others never should have entered the pastorate. Their contributions must be made in other areas of Christian service if objective analysis proves their destructive trends will not tolerate recommended therapy. Many such people are weeded out before graduating from seminary, either by advice from the staff or because they lacked the patience and self-discipline to finish their training.

We must be careful of our emphasis—our *over*emphasis— on outstanding competence. You cannot have a Protestant minister immersed in the interpersonal dynamics of a whole church, living as part of the emotions of all the people, and then place his head on the block for lacking the competence of a genius. Some churches with neurotic power structures go on igniting hell on earth for each minister while the denomination executive hopes just the right man will come along to turn the trick.

What trick? Infinite patience and inexhaustible love? This is no trick. This is the magnetizing nature of God raising all our spiritual levels. Love and patience are not commodities. For any man they are an epic of personal struggles, a record of a few more God-given victories than defeats, an enticement to have more of God. Our best of love is a thrust of all of us now and then, enabled by sweet grace and the prayers of our brothers. Does it seem to be something you can put on ministers' records in recommending them to difficult situations? Is it something to be measured by benevolence statistics?

Some men with more love and patience are sorry preachers and splendid administrators. Each man has a strong place in ministry, and together we long to sustain one another. Over the years, if we are patient with one another, we will all grow in patience. If we at least have faith in love, some of us can be more loving. But if we rate competence with a price tag in a dollars-hungry church we will breed hostility and fear. We will have smooth operations and little healing.

Together we must learn to minister to one another and absorb the rough-and-tumble shocks of self-discovery. If God's pastor is growing, then we can help him while he seeks to sustain us. Thus God's people will not turn on the prophet. They will follow him. When he is weary they will hold up his arm.

One last word about something that I think is terribly important—a sense of humor. One of the fruits of the Spirit is joy, and some adopted sons of our Father are even gifted with a sense of humor. This is a wonderful endowment. If one can see the humorous side of some bit of life, if he can come apart from the mainstream long enough to catch a glimpse of the winsome, the delightful thing, and if he can remember that there surely must be something beautifully cheerful in the heart of God to put up with us for so long, then I think he must be very close to that heart. His life must be like a flourishing tree in a dry land whose roots reach to hidden springs of faith. Others may be blown about, but he is steadfast. Others may carry the deep lines of worry, but his smile is like the assurance of sunlight. If God has given you that sense of humor, treasure it always. It is one of the gifts He will use to bring happiness to others.

8
The Spirit
Calls for Freedom

THE PRIMARY SUBCONSCIOUS TASK OF THE NEUROTIC IS TO
live with conflicting trends in personality by repressing them,
by suppressing one drive to live with another, or by compart-
mentalizing certain emotions to express one at a time. He
wants no part of internal conflict, nor any part of controversy
that will stimulate repressed trends and upset his inner balance of power. In business, politics, church and social life he
tries to become part of a calm situation (and he hopes it will
remain calm), or he depends on a strong authority or authoritarian person who will protect but not disturb him, or he
grafts himself into a power structure that is supposed to isolate
him from anxiety while it reflects his hunger for power and
prestige. Controversy can be tasted only if he is assured that
his power will be augmented and his safety insured.

The neurotic personality may find his goals impossible to
attain. He may reject society and its pains, and become a kind
of social hermit or beatnik. To most neurotic persons, however, this is an admission of defeat. Opportunities to realize
these goals are possible when he is backed by brute power (as
in the case of a dictator), or when a secure and socially accepted institution respects talents and values in which he
specializes. He may seem to be cavalier about the rewards
bestowed by professional and literary societies, churches, or
motion pictures, but he secretly lives for them. The hope of
respect, prestige and power is his life, his very breath.

The church, then, exists to provide tranquillity for him, to "sanctify" his neurotic trends, to provide a platform for the exhibition of his pride, to stabilize his personality structure, to bestow divine honors on his idealized image, and to disguise his conflicting emotions by letting him express them in theological jargon. He is at home among many other so-called "normal" persons who find in the institutional church a refuge from the distresses and conflicts of the world. To these people, the church should be as strong and reposed as the Rock of Ages, and anyone who upsets the calm conditions of a local church is looked upon with great disfavor.

This brings us directly to the problem of religious freedom. The Bible condemns internal quarreling, bickering, backbiting and slander. At the same time it promises controversy, conflict, suffering and tribulation in the world: "Woe to you, when all men speak well of you, for so their fathers did to the false prophets." While the church has God's truth, she must discuss, pray, study and ponder until she knows the application of this truth. And then, most likely, the world will reject it.

To know the truth and administer it the church must live and prosper in freedom. The church must understand and deal with neurotic personalities and power structures in her midst as a major step in enhancing her freedom.

In an age of intense anxiety, American Protestantism and American democracy paradoxically serve to augment anxiety and provide the salvation from it. Both are the products of the Age of Enlightenment's love for reason, but they are distinguished from other movements of that age by deep roots in Christ and Moses. Both make the maximum demands on man's resources and provide the critical test of his potential. Both the church in America and the state of the eighteenth century show their interacting influences in their historical documents.

Can man remove himself from the ancient landmarks (as Protestants did when they discarded most of the ancient symbols and traditions), face the cosmos armed only with truth, charge his neighbor and himself with deep and abiding verities, and then, of his own volition, retain his birthright of freedom? As Gerald Sykes says, "If America fails, as Freud predicted, it will be because the mind of man has failed." If man cannot live in freedom with only the truth between him and infinite nothingness, then he cannot live. If the Protestant man cannot live with his freedom, then the purposes of God have been thwarted now as in the Old Testament—and God, who has given us His Son, has nothing better to give.

The purposes of God *can* be temporarily thwarted, but not universally and indefinitely. Out of the church of our Lord will arise men who, by God's power, are willing to be free. Anxiety will always be with such a man. Each new trust in our neighbor and in ourselves opens up new anxiety. On the religious frontier of truth we do not have an authoritarian church to tell us what the truth is in every situation. We stand straight before God, taking the risks of responsibility. The loss of this freedom means that a light goes out in the world, even among reasonable men. In fact, the loss of freedom in the world, emphasized on almost every page of the New Testament, has produced a strange kind of general neurosis in culture. We have referred to it often. It is a general neurosis that produces classical neuroses.

According to psychiatrist Viktor E. Frankl of the University of Vienna, we are encountering the neurosis of "existential vacuum." The patient is sure life has no meaning. He feels it results from a loss of the instinctual security of the animal world on the one hand, and of social tradition on the other. "At present," Frankl states, "instincts do not tell man what he has to do, nor do traditions direct him toward what he ought to do; soon he will not even know what he wants to do, thus completely succumbing to conformism."

In the face of this alternative, the church must trust God so unswervingly that she can afford to live by the insights of courage. This implies that a democratic church (as well as a democratic state) must be operated successfully, even when it includes many who do not believe in it fully.

The neurotic personality does not trust himself. He does not fully know himself enough to trust. He does not see his neighbor as a person in his own right who deserves to be fully trusted. When he cries, "We want more freedom in the church," he is usually calling for the right to have temper tantrums without repercussions, or control of the church without discipline.

If the Protestant Church is to be truly democratic and truly an instrument of God's will, she must trust herself in fact. Her first consideration must not be doing away with those who fail to trust themselves, but providing maximum freedom for those who do. Even when the church is driven to exercise discipline, it provides greater freedom for the many and shocks the few into a new confrontation with their bondage.

To be her best self the church must forge ahead with the neurotic in her midst—and with the struggling psychopath, and with the backsliding saint, and with the overly aggressive pastor, and with the disagreeing and disagreeable theologian who may have more truth than we care to admit. To trust herself, the church must be able to think and act with discernment. This means sifting truth from error, right from wrong. She must be able to live with elements of error without the fear that they will automatically demolish the good. Her one requirement is that she be possessed of Christ. Thereafter it is not a question of what Christ would do if He were here; it is a question of what He will do through men because He *is* here. This is no easy question. To accept it, Christians must maintain an openness, attentiveness and a teachability in all relations with both church and culture— and especially before the open Bible.

Confidence under God strengthens the church to embrace those who, at times, do her great harm. The love of Christ enables us to conserve the best in all. The neurotic may make outstanding contributions on the boards, he may be an exceptional Bible teacher and do more visiting of the sick and shut-ins, and he may have brought many persons into membership. Then again, under conditions we have noted, he also may split the church and drive the pastor to a nervous breakdown. But the problem of striving ahead with disturbed persons reaching for the wheel is no different from the problem of doing the will of God through sinners. Indeed, we come right out and say we are great sinners. We know original sin. We all stumble and fumble and do the wrong thing without knowing the precise reasons. But we are forgiven, and we must have faith in ourselves and in each other because God continues to save us by His faith in us.

We cannot love unless God loves us. If the Protestant Church is to vindicate God's gift of freedom, she must be able to include all God includes. If she cannot absorb—indeed, *use*—the anxiety created by her own free condition in Christ, then she really has nothing to say to a sin-shackled world.

I have often pondered the popular contention that institutions tend to develop into their opposites. For God's witness in any stage of its reformation, this may mean the inability to absorb the anxiety of being different from the world and judging its sick culture. A free church then becomes tyrannical, and a church governed by the many becomes the institution dictated by the few. Once she forsakes a passionate devotion to the Christ of the Bible, the visible church begins a downward spiral accelerated by a subtle awareness of her neurotic condition: separation from her true identity and inability to undertake the mission dependent on that identity. The insecurities of the minister, the organization and the laymen are compounded. In the church this means that the organism becomes an institution that places more power in fewer hands while the people and pastor conform to the culture's standards of status and success.

We can perceive in these cultural standards society's disturbed response to its own anxiety. It is not simply that ministers "understand" these convenient values, but further, that they are in churches which have adopted these values, and are under the direction of disturbed persons who have incorporated these values into the pride system of neurosis. The more insecure we are, the more we tend to adopt some defense against threatening anxiety. The minister is not insecure because of his conflict with the world, but because of his conflict with his own church and his own conscience.

The insecurity of the minister is not hard to trace. Above him is the authority of the religious organization. Most of the denominational executives they meet are men who are dedicated to their work and who have made sacrifices in behalf of their organizations. Every minister, however, has met several executives at one time or another who have made a lasting impression of smug parochialism and organizational tyranny.

The religious organization grows, perpetuates and vindicates itself. Salaried officials must prove themselves by performance. Vanloads of promotional stuff are sent to the churches, so that one wonders whether the departments are justifying themselves to each other, or to the churches, or both. And the mammoth army of stationary engineers behind headquarters' desks grows every year. Ministers may not only be overcome by executive authority, they may soon be outnumbered!

Organizational men have their own insecurities. Each must prove himself to the men above him, and each needs the pastor to help him. The pastor is the workhorse who pushes benevolences, organizes brotherhoods whether he needs them or not, sends talented people to the city-wide administration, enforces the constitution, puts the latest ideas and memoranda into effect, works like an ant for special offerings, does splendidly on the special-day campaigns, rolls up his sleeves on the national stewardship propaganda, puts on a great fund-raising show for the capital-funds drive, and labors to put up, step up, without letup, in the name of God. He regrets deeply that lasting measures of denominational success must be translated into figures. Numbers measure size, growth and amount. By figures, one compares. By figures, rewards and admonitions are passed down.

The pastor is dependent on this organizational machine by dollars and cents. He buys bread from a salary dependent on the size of the church. To this money can be added prestige by placement on committees, trips to conferences, appointments to seminars (all expenses paid), or even by a choice job at headquarters. Sooner or later the pastor needs the kindness and tender mercies of the apparatus.

Below the pastor are the laymen in his own church. They are the ones who provide the figures, the talent, the work, the money—and the needed announcement every so often that "The man we have now seems to be doing a pretty fair job."

But the laity have their own worries. In their church work

they must prove themselves to families, friends, community, neighboring churches and, in a sense, to past generations. The church is the stage upon which they perform. Nothing so dampens their enthusiasm as poor attendance figures, no matter what the spiritual progress. They have learned to love dearly those well-attended events to which the culture may "come" and "participate," especially the Strawberry Festival, the Father-Son Banquet, the Annual All-Church Bazaar, and the Annual Fashion and Model Festival.

Laymen are engaged in the activism of what we might call the "theater concept" (which we will mention again in connection with Christian education). The theater concept of activism stimulates, and does not lessen, anxiety. Neurotic maladies are therefore aggravated because guilt is aggravated. American pastors themselves accelerate the pace of their activistic churches.

Activistic churches give the laity a Bible and proceed to tear it apart. They call people out of the sinful world and break their morale with an avalanche of worldly work. They invite souls on the pretense of exalting Christ and proceed to exalt pacifism, comfortable living, middle-class ethics, and salvation by world government. They challenge the people about the problems of race, economic injustice, and the struggle of the inner-city church deserted by the suburbanites, and then they do nothing on the assumption that if they have talked enough about a problem, they have done their Christian duty.

They invite people who have lost their identity and give them tenth-rate amateur psychiatry at no cost. They condemn Communism as being too materialistic, but when they get members they drain them financially for handsome parish halls of walnut, stained glass, plush furniture and expensive paintings.

They call to men, "Come unto me, all who are heavy

laden, and I will give you rest"—and they send these men into kitchens and committee rooms to run the Lawn Fete and the Fall Fish Dinner. The congregation has no time for evangelistic visitation because it is exhausted from doing "the Lord's work."

Activistic churches announce to the world that Christian citizens of democracy must outlive and outsacrifice Communists, and they proceed to sermonize on the three steps from rags to riches, and how to get rid of that Blue Monday feeling. No wonder Americans love to swallow verbal tranquilizers on Sunday morning! They are worn out from burning the church's candles at both ends. No wonder their neurotic symptoms are aggravated! They feel guilt with no atonement, fatigue with no peace, lostness with no direction, confusion with no foundation truth, and aimlessness with little sense of God's sovereignty.

Whatever the minister's qualms about identifying the Kingdom with an anthill, the denominational apparatus knows the layman has staying power and provides the funds. The church is using the denomination's materials, or it isn't. It is that simple. And if the pastor interrupts the layman's activism, and the latter becomes unhappy, he might go to the other church down the street. If this layman has been active in work up at headquarters, it makes matters even worse. Ministers in new mission churches feel this yoke even more. The denominational executive wishes to report to his superiors that the church in a short time is already self-supporting and using the well-advertised program materials in happy preference to Brand X.

Since the denominational power structure has its own interests to worry about, it does not take kindly to the pastor who does too much independent thinking or fiddles too long with Brand X. Either he is a company man, or he isn't. The power structure centered around the executive advertises the company's products loud and long, and they consider it a matter of financial and religious patriotism to punish deviation from the party line. When a layman goes to them and reports, "Our minister is too controversial and is upsetting the entire church. Giving is down," the pastor may be alarmed to discover how few friends he has at court.

It is a difficult thing to say, but there is often an evident feeling of suspicion and hostility among members of the cloth. They seem desirous of condemning anyone in a position they fear or look down upon, as if it somehow helped them. In conversation they quickly get to the subject of salary increases, incoming members, or projected and gigantic building programs.

They do not thoroughly enjoy each other's company, and cover their mutual distaste with the mellowed gentility of a condescending Kentucky colonel. When they do meet together, they do not really listen to one another. They are victims of St. Vitus' Dance, and carry over their vows of poverty, chastity and activism into their discussions. The laymen suppose that when ministers get together they discuss theology and philosophy. Little do they realize they are at their best in telling humorous stories, and acting rather normal when quoting the latest facts and figures, production and performance. Most ministers prefer to let their hair down with a golfing layman they can trust.

To this insecurity covered by feverish activism we must add the impoverishing element of theological liberalism. George Santayana said once, "A fanatic is one who, having lost sight of his aim, redoubles his effort." Nothing is so pathetic as the sight of a fanatically liberal minister keeping busy seventy hours a week. Some pastors have confided that their beliefs on cardinal doctrines are hazy or simply rejected.

These men would somehow like to see a better world, and in thirty minutes of powder-puff applications of patented happiness they will barely manage to make that hope clear. Dr. Norman Vincent Peale refers to them as the "would-be-erudite, superscholastic vocabulary-ish, ethical-implication, social-action type" who have "contrived an inordinate influence upon the church." During the week they are consigned to scurrying about for scraps of wood to throw on the altar of religious devotion in order to keep the jolly pot boiling. They may not be certain of what they can accept in the historic creeds, but they are quite suspicious of pastors who fervently preach a dynamic, life-changing expression of the old evangelical faith.

The pastor must contend with the needs of laymen as they see them (in addition to their real needs), with the demands of denomination and its power structures, and with fellow pastors aware of their insecurities and doctrinal undernourishment. He must contend with the downward pull of culture against his own prophetic vocation. And whatever course he takes, he feels he ought not to jeopardize the financial and spiritual well-being of his family. He must be what Christ calls him to be, and what all others expect him to be. And if he succeeds, he is really a failure!

Is it any wonder that the pressures on a sincere and dedicated pastor are often more than he can bear? If he is not independent in his thinking and true to himself, his conscience punishes him. If he defies the culture, society punishes him. If he fails to keep the local church's mutual-security arrangement in balance, the official boards will punish him. And if he begins to crack under the tensions, becomes slightly ill-tempered or hasty, everyone becomes impatient with him. The call to conformity becomes very appealing indeed, but the acceptance of it makes the abdication of the church's freedom a certainty.

In back of our prayers for some freedom for pastors and dedicated laymen is the hope for more and more freedom. Freedom is what the defensiveness of neurotic persons and power structures fear most, while it is actually the only hope for their salvation.

Opening arms to increasing freedom in the church will involve immersion in culture while maintaining Christian distinctiveness. Both neurotic influence (psychic idolatry) and worldliness erase this distinctiveness in defense against anxiety. But holiness, often prostituted by the pharisaic personality, guards distinctiveness, and rightly understood and practiced, makes for health and wholeness. Without true holiness the church sinks into culture's molds and cannot minister redemption.

Dean W. E. Inge wrote: "What is the main function of Protestantism? It is essentially an attempt to check the tendency to corruption and degradation which attacks every institutional religion. The general features of a religion are determined by the state of culture reached by the peoples who hold it. A religion as believed and practised cannot be far in advance of its worshippers. If a nation is progressing, its religion will become more enlightened and more ethical; if it is declining, its religion will lose its connection with conduct and will degenerate into formalism and superstition. It is difficult to say whether organized religion has on the whole done more to promote progress or to retard it. Its function is mainly conservative; it prevents gains from being lost, and abuses from being remedied."

There is now a debate on how much freedom the church is actually exercising and on whether or not she is doing the ministry for which she was commissioned. This is because on the surface the churches do a great deal of good. They may not be living on the moral frontier, but they are at least as good as the best elements of our culture. The condition of general goodness may exist for years because the culture is still riding on the coattails of the nation's bygone spiritual renewals. But already culture, spurred not only by its inherent illnesses but by the pressures and fears of our atomic age, is beginning a downward spiral. When the church follows it down, the world will once again be used by God to judge the church. Anxiety, like evil, contains the seeds of its own destruction; in the meantime the souls with a thin veneer of goodness suffer as well as blackhearted men.

Preventing the pure gospel from being altogether sucked into the institutionalizing process is possible if Protestantism asserts itself in "an attempt to check the tendency to corruption and degradation which attacks every institutional religion." Gerald Sykes uses the term "hidden remnant," and in the church we prefer the term "reforming remnant." The reforming remnant must be the total of the free prophetic forces that act as the heart and conscience of the church and mobilize the resources of freedom in behalf of the Word of God. It will include persons who have an eternal experience of the death and resurrection of Jesus, who have no private axes to grind, who have dealt harshly with their idols, and who are unafraid of persecution, financial loss or ridicule.

Because of the blessed hope of the second coming of Christ, the sovereign purposes of God have precluded the church's history from being a complete gamble. The Kingdom of God will come and His will will be done. At any point in time, however, the institutions of the churches may fail—and God has never left Himself without a witnessing remnant.

Today we do not always know where or through whom the Holy Spirit will choose to speak. In vast areas of the

·190·

church ill with anxiety, He obviously is being quenched. Rigid defensive systems contrived by man seek to shackle Him while professing to give God the glory. It is then that courage once again comes into its own. Said Sykes: "We know that man is more apt to become a fearful robot than a courageous individual. But we have also discovered that the courageous individual, even in a mass-dominated society, finally wins the most respect—though he must struggle, he ultimately wields the most influence." If we apply this to the Body of Christ we may say that considering her whole history, the church's glory is that freedom for which Christ set her free, and through which she provides the remnant prophesying an urgent Word from God.

The church has devised no way of guaranteeing how or when or where a Word from God will be truly proclaimed. She has devised ways of maintaining a certainty that it will not be proclaimed. In any stage of her life, enough of her sons can arise to restore the freedom that is requisite for the Word to be proclaimed anywhere. Thus, the church must be willing to listen. All of her children are sinners and the door is always open to repentance, but her harshest self-judgment ought to be reserved not for those who transgress the Word but for those who will not listen to it and will not permit others to hear it.

The Holy Spirit may be speaking in a fellowship of the Spirit. As Dr. Henry Drummond finished his address in Appleton Chapel at Harvard some seventy years ago, he said, "Above all things, do not touch Christianity unless you are willing to seek the kingdom of God first. I promise you a miserable existence if you seek it second."

Some men, like Dr. Samuel Shoemaker of Pittsburgh, feel that the most significant movement of the Spirit today is the drawing together of small groups for prayer, Bible study, discussion and commitment, with no purpose other than to seek first the Kingdom in their lives. The ground rules for these groups are discussed in Chapter 5. Any of the small books by Dr. Shoemaker, such as *Creating Christian Cells,* are classic.

What the Spirit is saying may be counter to our vital defenses and prejudices. Our subtle manipulation of the lonely dissenter may really be our rejection of the Lord's voice. We must be aware that our shock over what someone is suggesting in these groups may simply be our resistance to the "shock treatment" of the Spirit in breaking the anxiety-rigidity-conformity circuit. The radiant insight for the defensive sinner and the neurotic person is essentially the same, however arrived at—to converse with the Almighty, the soul must be naked before Him.

The Spirit may be saying something through the person taking the "wrong end" of a debate. He may be speaking through a "nuisance."

▨ ▨ ▨

In the involved sessions of the general meeting of a church, it became apparent that the governmental hierarchy of the boards and agencies was growing so complicated that few commissioners could understand exactly what they were doing and planning. The stated clerk had to stand in back of the moderator continually to offer advice and corrections. An irritated commissioner rose to his feet and inquired, "Could you tell me who is the moderator of this assembly?" The clerk bowed his head in what looked like numbed shock. The moderator censured the questioner. Many in the audience booed, groaned and stamped their feet. Quite a few actually hissed like children greeting the Saturday-matinee villain. It was interesting to guess how many of those who hissed subconsciously felt like the questioner. At any rate, if the Holy Spirit was attempting to speak to an institution about its government, He would not do so again through that embarrassed commissioner.

▣ ▣ ▣

The Spirit of truth may be speaking through another communion. The ecumenical movement often seems like the awkward regrouping of solid gold Cadillacs instead of a humble attentiveness to the Spirit in our brothers. For example, ordination often hinges on a correct attitude toward denominational materials. Ordination becomes doubtful if the one questioned suddenly confesses he might use the materials of another communion to supplement the curriculum.

In the New Testament the Jews were not about to admit that the institution of Pharisaism had much to learn from an uneducated Carpenter from nowhere. The damning question put to Nicodemus was, "Are you led astray, you also?" When a vindictive official of one denomination can think of nothing more condemnatory, he will whisper, "I'm sure he has Baptist (or Methodist, or Pentecostalist) leanings." The impact upon the pastor who has vowed to be courageous in freedom can hardly be imagined. The resigned neurotic personality cooperates in some essentials to buy off his independence. Dependent trends will succumb to blind spots and seek submission to the party line immediately. But the autocratic person has a tendency to criticize the oligarchy to the skies until he becomes a part of it. He then becomes a potentate without mercy, and the institution becomes the temple of his idol.

If the Holy Spirit cannot be shackled by our anxiety or bound by our petty schemes, He can be expected almost anywhere. Through our tribulation and peace, our atom bombs and our churches, through the lessons of yesterday and the experiments of today, He will again give us the Word as a sword. He will enable us to see the threats to our security as

·193·

the proving ground of His power. Our confidence in Him makes our ministry flexible.

This is a way of saying that our strength is within us, but it cannot be safeguarded in a human system. If our strength is thought to reside in a sacrosanct institution, then the people must be manipulated insofar as they are useful to it. Those with the greatest stake in the institution's success will be the first to equate the service of God with obedience to the denominational apparatus. Competence in healing sin and sickness in the church will be called for in behalf of the system, instead of as a means of glorifying God and enhancing man's freedom.

The pastor knows that the Spirit will not be bound. The Spirit may not choose to heal in the time or manner people have designated. Does this mean that with a statistics-conscious apparatus breathing down his neck the pastor and his people can work no faster than the pace of the Kingdom's most dissatisfied members?

It does not mean that at all. Where there is unity of the Spirit, men so bound by one purpose will forge ahead. The right of one or more to disagree is always respected. Each part of the whole will go in the light it has, while respecting the integrity of the others to take a different path.

The pastor is in a twofold ministry. He seeks the healing of the individual. He also leads the whole church on the bastions of godlessness. He does not always succeed with the individual, even though that one has influence with the world. He continues in his obligation to the Spirit working through all those who are healed and committed.

Healing for many with neurotic trends may never be the same as the norm described in textbooks. Some souls will have to live with suffering all their lives. And yet, by being caught up in the ongoing march of Christ in the salvation of other lost and dying souls, they may cover their illness much as one who once said that a messenger of Satan always buffeted him, but he rejoiced in the Lord always. Paul had a thorn in the flesh, but he also learned in whatever state he was therewith to be content. This is the salvation of men who die to the flesh and live unto God.

Was Hosea "normal"? or Amos? Or John the Baptist? Or Jeremiah? The question does not even make sense. We only know from the Bible that the fruit of the Spirit is joy, that Alexander the coppersmith acted "abnormally," and that those who were swept up in the will of God had a peace that passed understanding.

To lead the local church ahead when the witness of Christ is fighting for its very life takes courage and great imagination. The pastor may be led to work quietly in small witnessing groups, or he may do the bold, unusual, startling, attenion-getting, crowd-gathering thing. He may read Jeremiah and decide to say the hard thing, or he may look at Jesus and do the angry thing. In the Protestant Church he must be free to do it. His people must be free to respect him and follow his leading. To punish him because he does not conform to their prejudices is wicked. To call his good an evil within the church is sin against the Holy Spirit. And God will not permit this.

If the church will not protect and respect her pastors, and if the pastors will not band together to respect themselves and their calling, then God will step in and create a new vehicle of witness. He will abase some and exalt others. He honors His truth. His glory He will not give to any man or system.

9
The Authority
of the Word

THAT WHICH WILL SAVE MEN IN OUR DAY IS ESSENTIALLY WHAT will save the church: a rediscovery of the authority of the Word. A soul must have authority for what he believes, or he does not really believe it. To the soul caught in the shifting tides of insecurity the Roman Catholic Church appeals with its stress on infallible authority. The average Protestant has seen the Bible torn to shreds by destructive higher criticism. Slowly but surely his authority is becoming the structure and pronouncements of his denominational hierarchy.

An existential vacuum is sweeping our culture because the people have no well-founded system of beliefs about life and little authority for what they do believe. Disillusionment is rampant because science has been enthroned as the omnipotent god who reigns with some confidence over test tubes, and then raises more profound questions than he can answer.

The neurotic personality is possibly in the most hopeless dilemma of all: he demands the greatest safety and possesses the flimsiest authority for what he believes about himself. All his hopes are pinned on the authenticity of his idealized image, which exists intact solely in his imagination. He holds tenaciously to this phantom of safety because he can dream of no alternative. If he is in church, his first impulse is to request God to make His peace with his idol.

The only lasting authority that has provided the satisfaction of peace and wholeness has been the Word of God. The

Word is really the life and power of God which may be experienced by any human being. The Word is revealed by the Bible. It comes to us by the Spirit of the Lord Jesus Christ to whom we are directed by the Holy Scriptures. When anyone is lifted out of the kingdom of darkness into the Kingdom of light and love by the Word of God, he knows the Word to be abiding truth. In fact, Jesus called Himself the Truth. The Word of God opens the door to the eternal realities of God and the true conditions of man.

The self-validated authority of the Word makes for an inner peace which comes as the direct result of positive knowledge. Wholeness means peace, a reconciliation of conflicts through self-discovery and an allegiance of the total personality to the highest Power of all powers. The health or wholeness of God reconciles man to God. His holiness reconciles the intrapersonal conflicts of the spirit (neurosis), of the body (illness), of mind-body orientation (psychosis) and of the total personality in its relation to God and eternity (sin). Christ is our peace. The experiencing of His power now validates what we read in the gospels: that He did then, and can now, heal the sinner, the deformed, the psychotic, the neurotic, the psychopath, and all who are out of harmony with the fullness of God. "As it is, we do not yet see everything in subjection to him. But we see Jesus. . . ."

Let us repeat that the Bible is God's Word. Nevertheless, social institutions and pharisaic churches "in isolation" from culture may quote the Bible often and still not be receiving the living and sharp Word. In fact, the words of the Bible and the phrases of ancient creeds may be employed to raise the walls of an institution against the culture and its crying needs. The membership may actually adopt and "sanctify" society's defenses against anxiety within church walls while they deny any relationship to the outside and its evil ways.

·197·

More than one church hotly defends segregation while openly renouncing the world, the flesh and the devil.

The church "in conformity" with culture may adopt all the inventions and methods of secular psychiatry and sociology while translating a word here and there into Biblical terminology to make it more palatable in a hardening institution. It may really believe that culture itself has devised the best methods of healing its own illnesses and reconciling its own conflicts. In that case the church finds itself in the same dilemma as any unchurched person it seeks to redeem; the culture falls prey to its own anxiety because it knows of no authority greater than itself. One can understand why Dr. James I. McCord said, "And is it not equally true that the greatest weakness of Protestantism today is its slow but steady accommodation to culture and its gradual muting of the Word? For the Protestant minister the greatest sin is to attempt to bind the Word of God."

The tension between culture and the living Word is still best demonstrated in the New Testament. The culture of that day was saturated with religion and the words of the Old Testament. Jesus did not constantly quote the Old Testament in every breath. He employed the strokes of a deft brush dipped in the common life to give the world a glimpse of God's ways with men. Society was sure it could capture Him to fit into their concept of a Messiah who would glorify the culture *as it was*. Slowly but surely it dawned on those men that the Prophet immersed in their culture was the embodiment of a will opposed to the values of their religion-covered life. They finally murdered the Man, hoping to destroy that will. But the will continued in the Holy Spirit after the resurrection, and was attested to by signs and wonders. Behold! This was the will of God.

The will of God can be crucified by the culture it denies,

but its resurrection is the foundation of our faith. The Word also may be nailed to a cross and its disciples temporarily defeated. And if the Word is not raised we are hopeless, and our faith is vain. If Christ the Word is not the living Lord of life, why go to the trouble of cutting across the grain of society, no matter where it takes us? If, however, Christ is raised, then conforming to culture is not merely temporizing with the Word; it is an outright re-crucifixion of Jesus.

The preaching of the Word and the taking up of a cross go together. If the kingdoms of this world are not yet the Kingdom of our risen Lord, then conformity with culture is a renunciation of Christ and resistance to the Word. And, as we have witnessed in the New Testament, those who reject the living Word of God may be fanatically religious people.

If one is going to suffer tribulation in behalf of the Word, he must be sure of Christ in his life, sure of the eternal Life, and sure of himself. The foundation of his security cannot exist in his imagination. It must be so realistic that he is willing to be rejected by culture for a cause that seems to be failing, because he is sure of the resurrection of the Word. Rejection throws him harder on God, and he pins all his hopes on Christ.

I have long felt that those who richly embodied in themselves the rewards and values of culture as a means of glorifying and fortifying their weakened self-images fight the Word of God bitterly. When they do flee to the Word, they are overcome with rapture at the glimpse of God's gracious acceptance. Take for example two persons worlds apart, a man like the prodigal son and a man like Paul.

The prodigal son went all the way to embrace the epitome of secular culture. He had been exposed to the fire of the Word and could not extinguish it. He felt guilty about not quite measuring up to his community's demands, and guilty about rejecting the demands of the Word.

Paul went all the way to embrace the epitome of religious culture. But the Word was upon his heart, and never so much as when he saw the face of dying Stephen. Paul was torn in two by guilt. He knew he had never measured up to the perfection required by a culture that glorified law, and he fell far short of the Word.

We may think of many reasons why the prodigal son thrust himself into his position of terrorized insecurity. Paul confided that he knew from infancy he must be a pharisee of the Pharisees. But the neurotic personality presents a different case. His self-image is so idealized and unrealistic that he is forever in pursuit of a phantom goal. He has achievements to back up his claims, but oddly enough his real achievements often lag behind his potentialities. He desperately needs—no, *demands*—that culture authenticate his idealized image. His unconscious tells him he needs the reflected appraisals of culture more than he needs life, for without them he could not live.

The neurotic personality is not unlike the product of a religious culture. He is forever reaching for the unreachable, and seeking to attain the unattainable. He is forever laboring and forever weary, forever running and forever going in circles. If he hears the Word preached he assumes he is doing it, and runs that much harder.

What the neurotic cannot envisage is security without the plaudits of culture to bolster his flagging pride. He must be wrenched, so to speak—*torn*—by the Word from a culture that promises bread and delivers a stone. The Word must be forcefully, continually, sincerely preached in love for the message to get through that the unseen arms of God are everlasting security, and the platform of neurotic pride is made of toothpicks. If the local church becomes only another piece of culture—albeit a religious piece—it becomes increasingly difficult for the neurotic personality even to hear the Word.

In an age when men grab for any buoy in a storm, culture becomes more neurotic. It appears to be more sinful and more religious at one and the same time, and we ask, "How can there be so many church members and such a great interest in religion, and such a mad dash for hell?" But this is really an old story. Our predicament is not the fault of culture or Communism, secularism or socialism, bingo or the twist, the moon race or the rat race, the north or the south, Wall Street or Skid Row. It is the old story of abundant religion and little of the Word. "So the Lord cut off from Israel head and tail, palm branch and reed in one day—the elder and honored man is the head, and the prophet who teaches lies is the tail; for those who lead this people lead them astray, and those who are led by them are swallowed up."

The evil one has always sought to disguise his disciples as angels of light. He desires a progressive, reasonable, well-governed, thriving culture that is simply not under the government of Christ. He is happy for a boom in religion and a scarcity of the Word. He is satisfied with many religious persons who have no intimate and firsthand knowledge of the living God in Christ. And he knows that the neurotic personality is so reluctant to relinquish his hold on the idealized values of culture that even when he does flee to the Word he attempts to straddle two levels of life —one wholly dependent upon God, and the other to some degree dependent upon neurotic trends dressed in new garb.

Preaching alone will not help the neurotic personality, as we have noted. Many helps are needed. But the new wine will break the old wineskins, and the new patches of truth on the old pride system will tear off. Thus, unless the Word is con-

·201·

tinually and consistently lived and preached, the magnetism of culture with its cheap panaceas is too much with us.

We believe the study of the neurotic personality is of extreme importance. Failure to honor the Word will so aggravate neurotic symptoms that a final return to the humility, kindness, forgiveness and grace of the living Word entails crucifixion. There will be no great renewal sweeping the church today without an equally great price being paid. Occasionally God makes us pay that price when crisis, war and suffering strip culture's allurements and reveal its true worth to human security. At other times prophets arise and pay the price in behalf of many.

Today the church has her prophets. One can think of a dedicated preacher, or of the store clerk who lives next door. Both look cultured, wear presentable suits and have good manners. People like them, yet they have enemies—and more enemies within the churches than without. Their physical suffering is not great, but sufficient to evidence no compromise with the world if greater suffering were needed. They are involved in our times, sophisticated in our plight, held by God for their resources, and they stand against the tide of wasted existence that engulfs our neighbors. Both have their reward. Both are servants of the Word.

The authority of the Word, more than ever before, must be expressed in preaching, personal testimony, the sacraments and holy living. This authority must also be reasserted in Christian education, ordination, discipline and seminary training. To these we turn our attention.

10

A Ministry for Pastors

"AND HOW ARE THEY TO HEAR WITHOUT A PREACHER?" WITH that one question the Apostle disarms those whose faith in the Word is so attenuated that they are for throwing out the sermon. He affirms the place of preaching in God's economy as long as one man needs Christ. Men are redeemed by God's truth, and truth must be transmitted. Our day begs for the forthright declaration of the gospel as never before, for it is the power of God unto salvation.

Few men can so stir us on this question as Charles E. Jefferson, former pastor of the Broadway Tabernacle Church. He writes: "If a man has faith as a grain of mustard seed, he can perform wonders both in the pulpit and out of it. No one can preach well who does not believe in preaching. He must believe that it is a divine institution and that it is accomplished by supernatural power. He must grasp St. Paul's deep-rooted conviction that it has pleased God to save the world by the foolishness of preaching. . . . The Devil would rather have a minister do anything else than preach a sermon."

It was Dr. Ralph Sockman who said, "The churches today are better organized than they are pulpitized. The greatest need of the contemporary church is the strengthening of the local pulpits. I just happen to think that there's more need for strong preaching than for administration."

One may argue against preaching and point to much that does more harm than good, but the truth is simply that God has promised to follow the communication of His truth with power. When the Word is delivered it turns the wheels of history that much faster. Those who resist God's judgments need new proof of their security. Their feverish efforts give the lie to their secular creed. Those who will be saved look past the preacher to the empty cross and are introduced to life beyond culture. Preaching has been designed by God to realize His purposes on earth, and no method of therapy man has invented is less foolish in function or a fraction as effectual as the ancient means of dynamic communication.

We have discussed the power and limitations of preaching in bringing the neurotic to true being (see Chapter 6). I have witnessed neurotic persons brought to Christ through preaching. In all cases thereafter, continual progress in relations with people depended on the use of additional methods of the pastor's ministry, and especially counseling.

In listing the gifts of the Spirit, Paul invariably mentioned prophecy, which is a foretelling and a forthtelling of God's purposes in time and eternity. Prophets have been business men, carpenters, hermits, sheepherders, or anyone who received the call and plunged to the core of the supernatural and ethical elements of revealed truth. In their years of preparation they were courageous souls given to prayer, study and meditation, and were unencumbered by vested interests in traditional religion.

The prophet has had a distinct calling, and he relies heavily on the shafts of preached words to find the targets men hide so craftily. Today all Christians are prophets in their culture, yet not all have this gift.

The pastor has the function of prophet in church and community. But who is the prophet to the pastor, and to the hierarchy of the institutional church? One may argue that all paid servants of the church worship on Sunday morning and hear the Word. The truth is that we do not have many *outspoken* prophets speaking to the church, and those we have must be cautious.

If the leaders of the church had been constantly exposing their hearts to the prophetic Word, we would not be in our present condition. We would not have watched ourselves sit idly by while minor officials (and occasionally executives) pulled unscrupulous stunts in viciously persecuting brethren in a manner that would be regarded as despicable in the business world. We would not have suffered the embarrassment of watching secular organizations take the lead in social crusades repeatedly ignored by the church. We would not have stigmatized courage while glibly hailing society's standards of superiority and prestige as the only infallible rules for faith and practice.

The churches have thought about, but cannot seem to act on, the need for prophets to Christ's pastors. The pastors need what we might call the shepherd executive (area pastor), a man who is unencumbered by administrative details or a critical stake in the annual display of vital statistics. Some have referred to him as ministerial chaplain or *pastor pastorum*. Wherever possible we ought to oppose further complicating the existing machinery by the creation of more offices. Our present executives are business managers. They ought, instead, to be invested with the call and certification to the prophetic function.

Many elders could be installed as executive business managers in the field of administration. The area pastor would then be free to visit the ministers under his care, hear their problems, counsel them in marital tensions, and be the shepherd to them that they are to their people. This area pastor would be expected to give a sermon at least once a month at conferences or denominational meetings. Without being tactless, he could preach what needed to be heard from one who had been among his people.

In a disturbance that gets beyond a pastor, the area pastor could be called in, and could be of invaluable assistance to commissions charged with reporting on pastoral relations. Committees have utterly failed to do any kind of sound therapeutic reconciliation in local church disturbances. If anything, they succeed in inflaming already volatile emotions. Reliance upon the area pastor would certainly be preferable to the practice of dissident groups pouring out malicious hearts to another pastor who might be prejudiced.

It should be required of the pastor-executive that he have an excellent background in clinical psychology. He ought to have extensive experience in counseling in the local church, and he should be distinguished by wholehearted reliance on the Bible as God's revelation.

In choosing such a man the churches ought to avoid looking for a mild, timid, father-substitute whose chief claim to fame is that he has a friendly smile and gets along with everyone just fine. The church is filled with tacticians skilled in the art of pouring oil on troubled waters and we are all feeling quite slick, while our problems in interpersonal relations stay as sticky as ever. It is no disgrace to be tactful, but we are getting so skilled in compromise that we shall soon be indicting Christ for not handling that last Jerusalem situation a little more skillfully.

At times this pastor-at-large would have to be outspoken. He ought to be outspoken in his sermons. In private conversations he can keep pastors from going "shipwreck." Occasionally the local pastor comes on a counseling case with sexual coloring, involving himself or two parishioners. He may not understand it, and should feel free to call in his minister. In trouble revealing a deepening cleavage in the congregation the area pastor would have to spend hours in comprehending the fundamental interplay of conflicts of images. It is conceivable that after awhile he would make a few enemies. This development might come as a breath of cleansing air.

The area pastor might be approved for a limit of two terms, totaling, say, eight or ten years. In fact, we are very much opposed to servants of the whole church staying on in executive positions until retirement. The pitfalls of pompous authoritarianism are so painfully obvious that searching for enough men to avoid them for the rest of their lives has proved to be a hard task. How much better to borrow men from the rich experience of the pastorate, share their talents, and send them back to the local church with a new love for their ordained brethren. It would be a great experience for any Protestant pastor not only to serve his fellows, but to forget the need for raising funds, blessing bazaars and studying statistics like a Bible. He could gain an experience of the love of God that would humble him by its awesome vitality. Someone must come in the name of Christ to share the minister's burdens. Dare we subject our inflated self-images to the scrutiny of a man who claims to love us? Do we who preach the Word dare to open our own hearts to it? Are ministers as glad for the care of their souls as they expect their people to be?

While Paul considered himself the shepherd-guardian of the teaching elders under his charge, he still relied upon the Holy Spirit as the one true Vicar of Christ. One Spirit wrote the Bible, by one Spirit we have access to the Father, and it is one Spirit who maintains our unity in the bond of peace. The area pastor would have to believe deeply in the presence and power of that Spirit, and this belief would show in his care of those under his charge. If the neurotic personality claimed that the local pastor was unfit for his work, the church could be sure that the area pastor would seek the impartiality of the Spirit in searching and knowing the heart of the man called by that Spirit to his present charge.

The free church of our Lord is the open forum of God who speaks to the world. All our service, our labors, our love for humanity should stimulate this question: "Why are you doing this?" And the voice of prophecy thunders back, "We do it because God's suffering Servant has released us from captivity, and we bring this good news to you." Only that must have priority which lives God's love and broadcasts His Word. Whatever our church is doing, if it is not strengthening the hand of our prophets, we ought to ask why.

11

Discipline or Disorder?

THE APOSTLES AS WELL AS THE LEADERS OF THE REFORMATION considered a true church in Christ to be impossible without discipline. Discipline is the church's exercise of its Christ-given authority for the enhancement of its purpose, the preservation of its freedom and the cultivation of God's holiness. It is rooted in holiness and leads to greater holiness. It presupposes that both pastor and people are studying the doctrines conducive to holiness and are dedicated to a life of prayer. In the *Institutes,* John Calvin discusses prayer, fasting, congregational admonition and excommunication as components of the subject of discipline. Without the discipline of inner holiness taught and lived, the people reap the rewards of rampant subjectivism, and soon confuse liberty with license and freedom in Christ with anarchy in polity.

While churches today precede important meetings with jokes and feasting, Calvin affirmed that prayer and fasting were the proper requirements for granting the Holy Spirit power to do His holy work among us. When church officers understand holiness and cultivate it, they can be entrusted with the powers of judicial discipline. In this process the reputation and spiritual growth of the saints are protected. In dealing with offenders, its purpose is redemptive. Unless that is understood we shall continue to conjure up visions of inquisitions and ecclesiastical Gestapos when someone asks in bewilderment, "Discipline? In the *church?*"

Administrative discipline in the church has come into disrepute because denominations have disgracefully employed it to protect existing power structures when aggressive and independent pastors get out of line. Originally it meant the human administration of church government for the purpose of building up the saints for the work of ministry. We say "human" because discipline must be the work of church-ordained officers and pastors. Actually it is simply the authority of the Spirit in operation for the protection and guidance of the corporate body.

It is clear that all solutions for the sickness of the churches must work together. You cannot have Protestant freedom without authority. And you cannot have authority without discipline, which is based on spiritual renewal and the preaching of the Word and a sound doctrine of calling and ordination. And you cannot have these without a minister to the pastors and intensive doctrinal training in the local church. To have this, you must understand neurosis and neurotic personalities threatening church life, and then you must have the courage to call for new respect for the office and authority of the pastor. All work hand in hand. There is no point even in mentioning discipline unless you are willing to pay the price to upset existing power structures in the church, and unless you are willing to preach and teach the Scriptures, the catechism, and the confessions of faith with fervor.

The conflict concerning discipline reaches into our thoughts on the love of God. We often assume that love must permit the beloved to wreck the corporate witness of Christ's Body, or it really isn't love. On the contrary, discipline permits souls to respond to God's love without the punitive threats of others making a response well-nigh impossible. Here, for example, are two churches in America. On one Sunday the pastors of both preached on integration and the love of God for all men. In church A, the chairman of the board of trustees called a meeting of his friends and called for a petition to oust the minister on the grounds of disturbing the church's peace. The majority of members would have responded to God's love by integrating. The minister, however, left, and the church continued rigidly segregated.

In church B, the pastor and officers had decided to meet with the chairman and his friends in small cell groups for several months to talk things over and to air hostile feelings. Everyone saw the light and changed his point of view except the chairman. He felt that his authority had been undermined, his prestige lost, and that he had been purposely humiliated by the minister who, he thought, no doubt wanted one of his close friends to become chairman. He continued a violent program of slander and personal attack upon the minister. Pastor and officers finally called him to an official meeting, prayed with him, and gave him a letter of transfer to another church. When he left he took seven families with him. Today that church is integrated and the blessing of God is mightily upon it. Discipline made it possible for souls to respond to God's love and to do His holy will.

The church belongs to Christ, and not to those with the loudest tongues and most violent emotions. It would have been possible for the chairman of church B to repent of his slander, ask to remain in the church, and treat his brethren in love while disagreeing with their point of view. He chose to leave, hoping that would finish the church. The church, to his amazement, prospered, and he became emotionally and physically ill.

While our church has the desperate need to restudy and implement discipline, it is specious logic to assert that discipline precedes freedom, or vice versa. Both presuppose and are fed by the same spiritual conditions of personal holiness and the urge to witness to God's holiness and redemption. Let us see why this is so.

God loves the people of our culture and seeks to redeem them living and working in their society. It is not, however, frightening enough that our society is falling in a downward neurotic spiral of anxiety and conformity. The church has preached and taught the culture-goals of society as the will of God. The values of culture are the status-goals of the church, and these goals are tightly defended by the power structures of churches and denominations. As we have seen in this study, the church has tasted her judgment, and the world's anxiety has galvanized its values in these power structures through the idealized images of the neurotic personality. The very people who should be leading the church upward are the busy and prosperous-looking souls who yearn either to hide from the world in the sanctuary or to gain divine sanction for their neurotic trends.

To yearn for freedom means you long to become a part of the life-giving witness of the Holy Spirit to the world. It means you so trust God's freedom in you that you are engaged in trusting God's freedom in the world. But if, under a religious veneer—and often under a rigidly pharisaic veneer—you are perfectly accommodated to the spirit and values of the world, and even, to some degree, invest these values with neurotic pride, then you want freedom only to do what you are doing. If discipline exists in our churches today, it is not operative in behalf of freedom, but is exerted harshly from the other-directed forces of culture and from the inner-directed claims of the idealized image. Discipline exists in tension to guard and encourage freedom. When, however, spurious inner-directed forces guarding the integrity of the self-image are assumed to be the inner-directed work of the Holy Spirit, there is no tension between culture and church, between the images of man and the image of God, between discipline and laxity, and there is little redemptive discipline and almost no honest freedom.

You need a courageous, vital, personal unity with God in Christ to be free to go somewhere and do something in dedicated mission. And this is precisely what is required for the employment of church discipline.

Who are you going to call on for freedom and the return of discipline? The power structures that are the victims of the conditions they are spreading? Can the sick heal the sick? We are always wringing our hands and bemoaning our plight. "The church ought to . . ." shakes the rafters—and doubtless it ought to. We suspect that we come back to what we always knew: that man cannot save himself. Only God can save him. And the Spirit does not work everywhere at the same time and in the same way. We try to gain insight into our situation, that we might pray intelligently and work with God to see beyond symptoms to illness. If hearts are open, the Spirit will do a gracious work in our midst. Our fundamental therapy is not psychological. It is spiritual, meaning, "of the Spirit."

When we are submissive to the Spirit we can trust ourselves in the midst of tension. And the prophet will create tension. Pastors have discovered that they would call on their official boards to deal with destructive persons who did not respond to any of the therapeutic methods outlined in previous chapters, but unfortunately the board was the seat of the power structure. Pastors would appeal to the denomination, but it had its own power structure controlled either by expansive persons or fellow ministers unsympathetic with their interpretations of the church's mission. In numerous cases the pivotal personality in the church was part of the power corps of the denomination.

To whom can the pastor turn for help? This is an old question, and it explains why some of our best evangelists work independently, why many of our most courageous prophets and charismatic pastors move away from the control of the major denominations, and why we stress again the proposed office of area pastor.

In some of our denominations we have good judicial processes with ultimate appeal before outstanding minds of the church. But there can be no ultimate appeal in *every* case of prophetic men working against the downward pull of selfish, or frightened, or neurotic power structures. *The hand of the working pastor must be strengthened in every area of the church.* Where necessary, a courageous and farsighted denominational committee or an area pastor must first employ, with vocal and dissident church groups, the methods of psychological and spiritual therapy which in the past may not have been utilized. There are direct methods of drawing out individual negativism, and small groups of members may be created for this purpose.

When a committee from without the local church gives even the slightest appearance of being fair and constructive, it is able to assist the church in continuing her true prophetic function.

▨ ▨ ▨

After serving fourteen years as a Navy chaplain, Pastor Q. was called to his present church. Between twenty-five and fifty attended services. His predecessor had been ill three years and in some areas of ministry was inactive. Although this was a Presbyterian church, the board of trustees governed. Heavy debt hung over the congregation. The highest salary the former pastor had, after nine years, was $2,700, plus manse.

For over five years Pastor Q.'s ministry was marvelously blessed of God. Two morning services and one evening service were soon held, and in 1960 the church moved into a

$258,000 plant. Over six hundred members had been received.

A man who had been attending regularly, and who showed great promise, decided to join. He was soon elected clerk of session. It was discovered he was an ordained minister of the Congregational Church who had to resign from his last charge.

The new clerk soon opposed the minister on several points, overtly taking exception to his theological position. He planted the seeds of confusion generously. He took five other elders with him to denominational representatives and inquired how it would be possible to remove the pastor.

The complaints were:

1) People are not attending, and not supporting the church.

2) The church is in debt and there is too much stress on finances.

3) There is division among people and many do not like the outspoken pastor.

4) The minister is a dictator and is not tactful with members who drink alcoholic beverages.

The new clerk influenced thirty-five members into active opposition to the minister, out of a membership of 750. More and more it became apparent to everyone who viewed the situation with disinterest that he had designs on the government of the church without interference from the pastor. It was never determined objectively the extent to which the pastor considered the clerk a threat to his own position. But when the clerk was asked to preach a Reformation Day service in the pastor's absence he upset the congregation by going out of his way to take exception to the Biblical beliefs held by minister and people. And, of course, he knew the theological positions of both before joining. When someone goes out of his way to make theological differences the basis of church conflict, we must ask ourselves why, particularly when the parishioner could have joined any number of churches taking a doctrinal position compatible with his own.

An administrative commission was appointed by the denomination and it met for two years. In this time the chairman of the commission did not undertake any spiritual and psychologically sound counseling with the pastor. Neither he nor the commission met with him separately to hear him at length, to study his personality, or to see what he had done and how. The commission never sent a representative to the services to see how they were conducted. Privately some of the commission met with the pastor to advise him to leave. He made repeated attempts, but was sixty-one years of age and no church would call him. Slowly but surely it dawned on the dissident minority and its leader that the chairman of the commission was a spiritual minister and the commission had no intention of recommending to presbytery that the pastor be removed from his pulpit. With the congregation behind the minister, and with doors to the denomination now shut, the thirty-five withdrew and formed a Congregational church. Now Pastor Q.'s church is again thriving. It did have some difficulty in putting its finances into order, because of the large debt, and the commission made some helpful suggestions.

The commission's report said in part: "When they (the dissident minority) became aware that the commission was anxious to get to the bottom of the reasons for controversy in the church, and might even come up with suggestions for the removal of some of them from office, a movement was begun by some in the direction of withdrawing from the church."

▣ ▣ ▣

It is to be noted that this commission did not take the time necessary to study the subterranean interplay of conflicting images. They may not have had the resources to study neurotic trends and conflicts of self-images. Some commission members even took the common course of least resistance by privately asking the pastor to desert his field. But they had the scruples not to adopt this course officially as the fundamental means of bringing renewal to the congregation. When the dissident minority realized that its more vocal leaders might be asked to leave, they departed rather than face the church without the promise of regained prestige. If the Congregational church ever did flourish, it would already have a tightly-knit power structure with battle scars of corps devotion that newcomers could not soon match.

Each Baptist church is a sovereign body that links itself to other churches in a conference or fellowship. No such commissions are binding on the local church, but occasionally another respected minister or deeply revered executive is called in to intercede in conflicts. This was often the case with Dr. W. B. Riley, pastor and educator in Minneapolis and founder of the Northwestern Seminary. He advises fully trusting laymen to speak for the Holy Spirit in the government of the church, and when there are grievances, the man aggrieved should first go to his brother where they may deal with the matter on their knees before God. He speaks of the persons we have been discussing as "chronic trouble-breeders" and states: "Our mistakes are sometimes our best teachers. My own mistake in dealing with the trouble in the First Baptist Church of thirty-five years ago was to follow the advice of men and women who were too patient, too lenient."

He further advises pastors: "Only a few days since, I was called to counsel in another instance where a man and his wife had, for forty years, horned out pastor after pastor. I took the clerk's record and looked it over and could not find that any man remained longer than three years in that pulpit, and I found on the field two men who had been deeply gored by this horned deacon and his still more horned wife. I advised their exclusion, and it was accomplished. Time will tell if this also was wise!

"Let me repeat, it is a desperate act, and should be the last resort. But when it becomes clear that people have done nothing but breed discontent, write unsigned letters, anonymous letters (the lowest conceivable piece of conduct), get up petitions and, under false pretenses and by foul arguments persuade others to sign them; and, year after year, pastorate after pastorate, have proven themselves ill-contents, critics, slanderers of competence and character, the best thing that could possibly happen to the church is to remove them, and when the time comes for such action, and it is started, go through with it! Don't get cold feet; remove the cancer!"

Denominational discipline of pastors is supposed to be on the grounds of gross immorality or heresy, but it is rarely brought to consummation on those issues, as can be clearly witnessed by a study of the actual underlying causes of denominational discontent. On the one hand the people are told that mission and ministry rest with all redeemed souls; on the other hand, if the pastor fails to keep an insecure institution balanced on dead-center, he is disciplined. We have no objections to discipline *per se*; we have simply perverted that discipline on which the Holy Scriptures dilate. The layman has come to feel that it is his exclusive protection against a prophet who threatens him or his position.

If the layman who refuses therapy and sows seeds of scandal, slander and malevolence in the congregation were to be disciplined, the church of Jesus Christ would no longer be treated with becoming the private club of the cream of society. Both church and world would see that the Body still speaks with the authority and mind of Christ. John Calvin clarifies this point: "And that no one may despise this judgment of the Church, or consider it as of little importance that he (the disciplined offender) is condemned by the voice of the faithful, God has testified that it is no other than a declaration of his sentence, and that what they do on earth shall be ratified in heaven. For they have the word of the Lord, to condemn the perverse; they have the word, to receive the penitent into favour."

A complete misunderstanding of discipline contends that Christians ought not to judge one another. Discipline really is an authoritative expression of the church's supervision of her purity and servanthood. It is often the only effective means to correct vindictive and continual judging by a dissident minority. Discipline puts individuals on notice that the church will not tolerate the persecution of the pastor or any of his people by a small minority that sets itself up as an independent and self-sufficient judge of moral behavior.

The church seeks to discipline herself that the world may not judge her and find her wanting. Discipline never considers its mission completed until the church rejoices that the offender has come to a decisive step of self-understanding, and in repentance desires to serve the Lord selflessly. In this approach of sincere love the church may then learn whether she has failed in any way to minister to the restored son. In true discipline the whole church as well as individuals have something to learn from our Lord.

One question remains: What happens when the executive or the area pastor discovers through repeated interviews that the local minister is disturbed? Getting him off someone's hands by sending him to another church in that condition, or worse still, casting him adrift to wait for another ship to happen along, would never occur to a true disciple of the Lord Jesus Christ. The denominational committee dealing with ministerial relations will usually have to accept the counsel of pastor-executive and inform the local church that as the minister assumes the redemptive care of his people, occasionally the flock must assume care of their shepherd. No doubt this would entail a leave of absence of several months while the pastor receives professional counseling and spiritual nourishment, either in that city or in a church-related rest center. And the denomination that regularly sends down astronomical askings and grandiose programs should have no hesitancy in assuming the church will continue to provide full salary. Thereafter, if the pastor senses that he cannot minister in his field with confidence, at least he can wait upon the Spirit for another direction instead of fleeing at gunpoint.

We say that we apply discipline by suspending members who absent themselves from the life and worship of the church. Actually, members generally feel that the pastor is to do the church's work of ministry, and when church isn't booming he should be punished. We all know examples, however, of the church exercising self-discipline. When supply ministers substitute for an ill pastor on leave, the Spirit often leads the people to take hold, and they discover they can do many tasks which they previously let fall on the shoulders of a few. When the pastor returns, they demonstrate the fruits of discipline in self-respect and encouragement of their leader.

Church discipline is not required for the safety of any one person or for the security of an introverted power structure. It is required by the Spirit working through love to enhance the life and witness of God's servant people. Since it presupposes other conditions in preaching, Biblical theology and Christian education—all combining to stimulate a new awakening to God's sovereignty and the church's servanthood—it must be reiterated that no one prescription can now solve all the church's problems and no one medicine will suffice for all her ills.

12

Prayer
Is a Major Subject

IT IS NOT TOO DIFFICULT TO UNDERSTAND WHY PROTESTANTS are caught in contradictory attitudes toward their pastors. The "priesthood of believers" can only stand on its two feet when it is trained to pray and is taught sound doctrine. Pastoral weakness in theology has revealed strange attempts to make the pastor a slick high priest in a talkathon stage play called, *Let's Us Good Folks Go to Church*. He is the center and we don't think he should be. We all should be at the center, serving God. But this presupposes a taught and committed servanthood—which is glaringly lacking.

Instead, theological gratitude to the grace that motivates good works is replaced by haphazard and whimsical appreciation of the minister's competence, social calls and personal service. But when the show drags its feet because we lean on a weak human reed, we downgrade the importance of the pastoral ministry and undercut the authority of those who are honestly doing a good work for Christ. As the New Testament is reread we can see that it is not a question of either-or. We pray for the church's revival and renewal. We also pray for the training of more competent pastors.

Dr. Roy Burkhart said that he had numerous opportunities to counsel pastors in private and small groups. Too many are filled with resentment, envy, frustration, worry and hostility. Some confess to not being born again, and many to not living before the throne of grace in prayer. Dr. Burkhart proposes deeply spiritual seminary training.

Ministers still have the most influence in encouraging other young men to receive God's call. The image of a respected pastor lingers with new ministers. We know cases wherein some students did not enter seminary because of disappointment in evaluating the skills, mental attitudes and accomplishments of their pastors. Some pastors have actually discouraged others from entering the ministry because of their cynicism over the weakness and conformity of the church. But if the church is going to change, we shall have to work heroically with her future pilots.

The Episcopal Church has the most advanced program of psychological testing for students thinking of the pastorate and related ministries. The psychiatric staff of Cleveland Clinic tests hundreds of Episcopal students every year, once before entering seminary, and again three years later. Findings go to the bishop who studies the Clinic's evaluation. There is no correlation of behavior with other tests or other follow-up after graduation, although the bishop may recommend counseling at any time on the basis of the test data.

In the Clinic, a short social history of each student is recorded, and each is given the Wechsler Adult Intelligence Test and the Minnesota Multiphasic Personality Inventory. The latter tests neuroticism and other areas of abnormal behavior in nine categories, such as hypochondriasis, depression, hysteria, paranoia, etc. It is a good test with four validity scales intended to expose records that are difficult to interpret because of deceptive or evasive answers. The Rorschach Test is given for major checkpoints in normality.

The Draw-a-Person test (Machover's adaptation) is often used. It detects perfectionism and rigidity. Can students accept guilt, failure in themselves, obvious shortcomings? The overall patterns are the same for the general population. Tests of the students, however, revealed slightly more tendencies towards perfectionism, plus a number of "drifters" who were not sure what they wanted in life. The MMPI revealed a generally heavy weighting of femininity in interests (not homosexuality). Not more than five to seven per cent of the testees were poor risks psychologically.

Dr. Harry DeWire, head of the Department of Christian Education at the United Theological Seminary in Dayton, Ohio, finds these factors significant on the group profile:

1) A feeling of inadequacy and even inferiority; pronounced doubt about masculinity, and therefore some fear of relationships with other persons, and some tendency to be basically a passive person.

2) Some tendency to overstrive in interpersonal relationships.

3) Some hostility and resentment toward authority in the subculture (community) in which they were oriented.

4) The tendency to defend against these unwanted feelings. Most of the preministerial students expected to improve their prestige in the home and community. These findings agree with other test indications that some students feel they will not have to work very hard in the pastorate.

At Cleveland Clinic, when the testing is finished, students go to the office of psychiatrist E. M. Zucher. He first notes the Wechsler test for any disparity between verbal and performance results. He often plays it by ear, asking questions based on information offered by the student: "What motivates you to go into the ministry? What was the reaction of your relatives? What about your sex life? How concerned are you about your health?"

Dr. Zucher stated that an atheistic psychiatrist would not be good in interviewing, in his opinion. He added, "I would not feel right in doing this if I were not a Christian."

When I questioned Dr. Zucher about anxiety as a liability, he said that minor neurotic traits should not in themselves be disqualifying factors. Almost everyone has some neurotic tendencies. Dr. Zucher went on to say that a person who is sensitive to some anxiety has a good lever prodding him to act. The aggressive type, with a boundless source of energy for leadership and administration, may be excellent in some areas of the ministry, although he may antagonize some parishioners. Dr. Zucher concluded that no psychiatrist should have the last word. He can help point out traits, but the seminary staff and its own psychologist should have more to say as they observe the students from week to week.

More and more clinical preparation in the seminaries is being recognized as imperative. This involves pastoral work in hospitals, institutions and churches, with supervision and evaluation by chaplains and seminary staff. The important point is to integrate this work with classes in theology and small group discussions. Without this concentrated background in theology we shall continue with recipe and "how-to-do-it" courses in sociological humanism for a society already benumbed by the herd's circular stampede.

By far the most adequate college program is one that gives the student as much training in psychology as he can get. Seminary should continue this with courses in pastoral psychology.

The middle seminary years should allot one day a week for actual pastoral work among patients mentally and physically disturbed. This series of perplexing encounters will force a student to think through his own beliefs. If the Holy Spirit is directing his work, he will undergo a change himself.

If the ecumenical movement progresses, merging churches

will free us from the wearisome futility of "the small friendly church" and will call for more specialized ministries. We shall be driven to require an internship of one year on the field before the final seminary courses. Ten years in the ministry have taught me some questions I should have been asking in seminary. Let us say they were being answered and I wasn't listening.

We rarely realize that seminaries are under anxious stress and often under the iron thumb of power structures of their own. They seek a certain prestige by setting the fashion in theology, and they communicate with each other over our heads by an ultra-high-frequency vocabulary. Why do they continually use men who have not been in the pastorate in ten or twenty years? Why are so many of our students pressed into the institutional mold even before they accept their first call?

Our students ought not to be invited to ministry; they should be recruited. Not coddled, but trained. Not chatted at, but indoctrinated in fundamentals. Not talked at, but worked with. Not entertained by a visiting brilliant speaker, but thrown for awhile into some dying excuse for a church in the basin of the city. We are producing a bunch of discussers instead of a brotherhood of inspired fighters. And they go into churches where the high-flown program materials are always asking the people to make clever interpretations of a faith they little understand and a doctrine they have never been taught. The members are so afraid of being called fundamentalists that they do not know the fundamentals they are supposed to reject. And the new pastor is sophisticated about what fashion dictates rejecting, but not about what faith keeps demanding.

It is to the everlasting credit of some of our most committed students that they consider prayer as vital as any course they study. How well I remember the phrase of Dr. W. W. White, which my own seminary would not let me forget: "Prayer is work, prayer works, and prayer leads to work." I look back, ashamed, to realize that dry-as-dust, late-hour discussions of divine sovereignty versus free will usurped valuable time that should have been devoted to prayer and time alone with our Lord. But students who remained constant in prayer gained renewed power. They were students of theology. When they went into their first church and took life's postgraduate courses in neuroticism, boredom, loneliness, sin, constitutional psychopathic inferiority, and alcoholism, their prayer life gave them an anchor of hope when other young pastors were being tempest-tossed.

The pastor never stops growing. With their calls, some churches stipulate that all their pastor's expenses will be paid for one week a year (in addition to his vacation) for the purpose of attending some conference. This permits him to spend time in spiritual re-creation and in regaining balance. In sharing burdens, pastors can cleanse their humanity and appreciate the sympathy of the Son of man. They can learn to love again and be more like the Son of God.

13
Of What Use Is Ordination?

GOD REACHES INTO THE CONTINUOUS STREAM OF LIFE AND calls out individuals for specific tasks. Once weighted down with the heavy responsibility of his calling, a man wonders that God should entrust so much of importance to sinners. What husband is sufficient in himself to hold the great happiness a woman entrusts to his keeping? What father should have the power to mold the minds and souls of his children before they are capable of making their own decisions? Perhaps God should not have such faith in us. Who is worthy for these things?

And yet these responsibilities fall upon us by the grace of another. A man suddenly finds himself in love. At that point he has no idea how heavy life's responsibilities will be. But all of life was meant to lead him to God. If he has the Lord's leading and grace to measure up to his tasks, he lives in the flow of life's grandeur.

It is this way with ordination. God reaches down and calls a man to be a shepherd of His flock. Who is worthy or capable to enter so deeply into men's souls and bring them God's Word? No one, obviously. It is His grace. There is never a day when the minister does not know how much he needs God for his calling. And he cannot begin a day without the assurance of God's forgiveness for having stumbled the day before.

It really is a strange thing these days to hear what ministers (not laymen, mind you) are saying about their own ordination. They are unhappy. They feel that we ought not to have pastors over the flock. We ought to abolish the clergy (I hope merely by dismissing them!) We ought somehow to ordain the laity and fire the clergy so that everyone will go into the ministry. They assume the misguided laymen think the pastor is somehow above them. Who is worthy to be a pastor? No one. So the reasoning goes.

But the laymen are getting this new message. The chairman of an administrative commission was saying recently that the leader of the dissident minority stated, "There isn't any difference whatever between laymen and that minister of ours. Who does he think *he* is? The laymen are the bosses, and pastors are no better than the rest of us."

The words were true enough. A father or husband or president or pastor is not inherently better or worthier in God's sight than the rest of men. Ordination manifestly never placed a fellow Christian on a pedestal. But this layman was interpreting current propaganda to its predictable conclusions. Where does this propaganda come from, and why?

Wherever you have a confluence of thought, you have a mainstream of cure-alls. Today there is a sense of frustration among the clergy, disappointment at the number of laymen who refuse to minister in Christ's name, and a loss of confidence in the power of preaching the Word. The world is moving at supersonic speed while the church plays games with culture and serves tea to herself.

Our leading thinkers are sure we must do something. As Emil Brunner said (*The Misunderstanding of the Church*), the *ecclesia* must find new modes of ministry and fellowship within and beyond the institutional church to capture the ear if not the heart of this generation.

Some extreme liberals have their remedy handy. They want

to do away with ordination to the holy ministry and to stultify preaching. Their selling point is that by downgrading the pulpit you will elevate the pew, and the moment the layman hears that there are no more ordained pastors he will run out and reconsecrate himself to full-time Christian service, prayerfully rejoicing, "Thank God, *that* obstacle is out of the way!"

The argument seems to be proved by negatives. Could not some laymen preach well? Yes. Could they not conduct the sacraments impressively? No doubt. Could they not visit the sick? Certainly. Aren't some laymen as capable as pastors in administration? Unquestionably. Well then? Get rid of the clergy, and laymen will step in and do their work.

Now, in the freedom of the church, the Spirit may be speaking at any time, and that is why we must be attentive to any idea, no matter how it strikes us at first. So then, John L. Casteel says: "The church must surely proclaim the Word of Reconciliation to all men. But this may or may not mean that we continue the practice of delivering at 11:26 every Sunday morning a discourse compounded of Biblical allusion, practical moralities, and wild surmises, by some one who has been 'set apart' and charged with authority to 'preach the Word in the congregation' [in, note, not at!]—a cultural configuration derived as much or more from Greek rhetoric, Stoic practice, agrarian time-tables, and the fashions of a 16th century Geneva gentlemen's overcoat, as it is from any theological or scriptural warrant."

The only trouble with this argument is that the Apostle Paul would have been the first to agree with most of it. There is a foolishness about preaching in that weak men with a poor knowledge of the Word set about to so speak that men will forsake a pattern of life and turn to God. To say that God would stoop to using such a method and such a human instrument seems to reflect somewhat on the Almighty! This, in effect, is what the prophets were thinking when they received their call: "Why, Lord, if you are down to me, you are scraping the bottom of the barrel." The men who led us pastors to Christ and those who trained us for our tasks no doubt felt the same. "But we have this treasure in earthen vessels, to show that the transcendent power belongs to God and not to us."

This fact from Scripture is a good answer and a great consolation. In fact, I must smile now and then at it all. Considering the way I sometimes minister and the way I preach, when a soul finds victorious power in Christ there is never any doubt in anyone's mind that all of the glory is God's.

The New Testament is fully aware of our predicament and utter dependence upon God. It states that the church has been given the office of pastor (bishop, teaching elder). Strict requirements are laid down for this office, and the pastor is to build up the saints for the work of ministering. The culture is to be confronted with the Word of God from every believer, not solely when a local pastor speaks at a Parent Teacher Association meeting.

The pastor is to be a shepherd to the flock, he is to preach the Word without fear or favor, and he is to administer strongly so that sinful or neurotic persons do not accept important nominations before they can benefit the whole church.

The pastor is a counselor but not a psychiatrist, a student of the love of God and one who apprehends the Book and its promises. He is, above all, one who recklessly launches his heart upon a sea of human need, and spends himself extravagantly in retrieving shipwrecked men.

Wherever he goes he symbolizes both the local and holy catholic church. He presides at the communion table so that in the minds of laymen he may represent the presence and participation of the whole church.

Here then is an office of the Spirit. Some men receive this call and accept it. Having been duly satisfied of his call and acceptance by the church, fellow Christians certify the Spirit's work and their approval by the laying on of hands. Thereafter the pastor does no other work but that of ministry to people in Christ's name. Ordination, like marriage, signifies new relationships, new work and a whole new body of responsibilities. Does anyone for a moment seriously believe it makes the pastor a better or more favored person?

Unconsciously, the disturbed person, or one with a severe inferiority complex, may wonder if this is so. We have noted elsewhere that the pastor is a distressing element to these persons. But this is not a problem we are at liberty to settle (if we could) by reducing the authority and leadership of the pastor. The conflict lies within the disturbed person. A situation in which he is actually and officially the leader, without interference, is too threatening and frustrating. On the other hand, he is continually worried that the pastor is becoming a dictator. He is threatened by a pastor who is overly aggressive. Unless he has trends of morbid dependency he prefers a resigned or masochistic pastor who glories in persecution and suffering. The neurotic's problem is not with ordination, but with himself.

It is, to be sure, a serious matter when in the eyes of culture the pastor is looked upon as the most important person in church, if not *the* church herself. The culture no doubt feels it has immobilized the church by turning the preacher into one swell guy. By this is meant playing golf with him and swapping stories at the local Club luncheon.

The restoration of the pastor's true New Testament role will come about when both pastor and people rediscover the authority of the Word. The problems connected with ordination could be solved if the Word were touched with the fire of devotion to Christ, and if our prophecy and Christian education first inculcated a well-defined system of evangelical doctrine. Then our people would know what and how they are to minister in Christ, and there would be a rapport between shepherd and flock within the freedom of the Body. Every soul would know himself to be a minister without feeling that the pastorate offered too much competition.

Our problems concerning ordination show that we are attempting to convince laymen that they are the true ministers of Christ, without undergirding them with the authority of the Word. We neither preach the Word with fervor nor call for life decisions. Consequently, when culture is absorbed into the church, the laymen work unwearyingly at trivia which they are told is "ministry." The pastor seems to be the only one doing the praying, Bible reading and talking about God. Is it any wonder that neurotics think he is some threatening distortion of God, and that the rest of the church looks up to him on his holy pedestal?

In many churches "in conformity" you find an idealization of the pastor. There is sweeping identification with him. He practices enough religion for everyone. If one doubts this, read the minutes of the official board. We have read the minutes of numerous boards given the responsibility of guiding the spiritual growth of the Body. This set is doctored up a bit, but here it is in essence:

▨   ▨   ▨

Meeting opened with prayer by pastor. Minutes read and accepted. Committee reports given, and the music committee reports the organist requested additional funds for music. The matter was sent to a committee appointed by the music committee, composed of two members of the board and two trustees.

There was a question of whether the benefit card party should be under the direction of the stewardship committee or the fellowship committee. It was decided after much discussion that both committees should meet jointly, with the chairman of each presiding alternately each month.

The petition of the board of trustees requesting that Boy Scouts be restricted to the small fellowship hall of the Christian Education Building was read, and on adopted motion it was voted to reactivate the position of Institutional Representative, and that this person (whoever he is) look into the matter and report back to this board through the clerk.

Mr. —— suggested we do something official for Mr. —— and his family in honor of their son's appointment to West Point. It was voted to have a silver tea in the Upper Room reception hall, sponsored by the women's association, on Friday, March 16, at 8 P.M., with the entire church invited. It was voted to give the bill to the board of trustees to be listed in expenditures under "session fund."

The pastor asked if there were any ideas or suggestions to benefit the spiritual life of the church. Mr. A. called to pastor's attention that his sermons have been running five or six minutes overtime. The pastor said he would try to correct that. Mrs. L. suggested we use live flowers on high and holy days. A lengthy discussion followed on what constituted high and holy days. It was finally decided to set up a program in the fall for procuring flowers for the altar for special days. The Faith and Life Committee was given the task of recommending whether artificial flowers may also be used in the sanctuary.

The pastor suggested the board look into the matter of nonactive members, but due to the lateness of the hour it was decided to postpone that question to next month. Meeting adjourned with prayer, and a time for coffee and fellowship followed.

In other minutes like these the pastor does not inquire about inactive members. He argues as long as the next fellow about whether the new drapes should be blue or green. When he becomes a cultured business manager and genial, all-around host, no one sees much difference between what he is doing and what anyone else could do much better. Consequently ordination becomes a nice affair without too much understanding of what it really means.

If the pastor is leading the way in discovering and living the authority of the Word, the ordination of laymen will have new meaning. It ought to be the goal of every church to train every member for service on the board of deacons. This is an historic board showered with honor in God's eyes. It is a group of Christians with one thought: how to serve Christ in any task, no matter how menial, wherever the church calls and there is need. The deacons are committed to pray with the sick, write to the burdened, visit the lonely, serve tables, minister to the poor, and *do* whatever needs to be done.

If the neurotic personality is making progress in maturing interpersonal relations, he ought to begin service on this board. Usually he will not think much of it because his eyes are on the board of stewards, or the council, or the session, where the *real* prestige is to be found. But the church will begin preaching a powerful message to the world when she honors service instead of serving those with honor. Most of the church business now discussed so soberly and lengthily by the other official boards should have been turned over to the deacons for action. But if you stripped official boards of discussion about drapes, and left them with matters solely pertaining to the Word and its ministry, silence would reign and prestige would depart.

If culture could not serve silver teas in the house of God, it would have to let the church be the church. Instead of laymen trying to get on the board of trustees as the next step to status, they would serve on the board as an avenue of ministry. When ordained persons, clergy and laity, are concerned with serving God instead of serving themselves, they are less concerned with the status ordination confers and more with the sacrifice it requires.

Let us have done with the business of discussing the abolition of ordination as if it were the key to turn *the* miracle. The *great* sacrifice begins in reordering our thinking, destroying our chrome-plated idols, and permitting the Spirit of God to talk sense to us. The sacrifice calls for a basic evaluation of our goals and self-images, and an honest admission of how much faith in the Word inspires our ministry. In the spirit of this sacrifice, both pastors and elders can honor their ordination and share the administration of Christ's church with openness and teamwork.

The sacrifice acceptable to God is a contrite spirit. It will take more than talk and social pronouncements for church members and clergy to extirpate their hidden motives of superiority and prestige which have married the church to the world. It will take a humiliation of self in the example of Jesus, and those who are willing to be abased will be exalted by God.

▣ ▣ ▣

In the Sunday morning service I had described a home I visited. The house was filthy. The father was on a drinking spree, one child lay helpless with muscular dystrophy, and the mother was bedfast, dying of cancer. I related how the whole room seemed to light up when the young child led us in prayer. She had a few sentences for their home, but most of the prayer was for my work and her church. The illustration had to do with prayer and faith.

Later that afternoon, Mrs. N., a church member, knocked

on our door. She had not been very active, and seemed to some to be rather proud and aloof. Of late, though, she had been showing signs of apprehending the grace that was hers in Christ. She stood in the doorway, dressed in an old shirt and blue jeans. I must have looked a bit surprised. She wanted the address of the home I had mentioned in the sermon.

I walked Mrs. N. to her car. Before I had a chance to ask why she wanted that address and what she was going to do with that pitiable family, I saw soap, rags, mop and bucket in the back of the car. I remembered making a point in the sermon that any prayer not offering self as the first means to answering its petitions is not entirely sincere. That afternoon our people were thinking how wonderfully God answers prayer, while Mrs. N. was out scrubbing walls and floors in the name of the Father, the Son and the Holy Spirit. Mrs. N. began to show some of the requirements for a deacon, which are the same requisites as for a Christian.

14

Education on a Merry-Go-Round

THE CHRISTIAN LIFE IS BASED ON TRUTH, NOT ON FANTASY. IT is entirely realistic, not the product of illusion. Its heart is not the idealization of the images of man, but restoration of the image of God. It is not an imaginative reproduction of the symbols of the racial unconscious, but the facts about Christ and what He has done for us sinners.

Other religions have created a body of convenient beliefs like a handle with which to turn the world around to a more comfortable position. Not so with Christianity. It is historically accurate and metaphysically valid. Its truth is spread before the eyes of the world, and its promises are open to the world's testing. The Truth Himself marched up the world's roads because His disciples were certain that Jesus really was God, that sin really was paid for in the cross and resurrection, that the Christ-life is really the one God had in mind for all men, that Christ really did rise from the dead, that there really is a heaven and a hell, and that Jesus is really coming to reign on earth some day.

No wonder that the Lord told His people to spread the gospel by teaching—not to spread it by indiscriminately transcribing names to a roster, by forming joint study committees with the government, by accepting the kingdoms from the devil's hand, or by aping culture to become popular. Instead, we are to spread it by making learners (disciples), baptizing them into God's family, and teaching them to do (to observe, practice) *all* that He commanded us.

When the church is not sure of the truth and loses her desire to spread whatever she does have, then she cuts herself off from involvement in society's real needs. She does it by closing off a bit of society within her walls and mimicking culture under her terms. She weaves a piece of the world into a religious tapestry.

The worldly activities within the church reflect the theater concept of religion. You go to the show and pay for it. If you are important in the world, or would like to be, you go into the acting and production ends.

Here the pastor is the director and there are many producers over him and many assistant directors responsible to the producers. When the show is a flop the director must take the blame. When it is a success everyone must take a bow. A good show is one that gets rave notices, makes big money, packs them in, puts on a consistently good performance, and brings the talent scouts down to sign up the stars for bigger and better things.

In the theater concept of religion, education conditions children and adults to activism. The pastor thinks up clever gimmicks in the way of little songs, tags, hostesses, sensational signs, happy recognitions, and gobs of saccharine sentimentality. The children cut out dolls, color dolls, dress dolls, and paste dolls—all in preparation for the time they will work on paper dolls in institutions for the mentally ill.

Meanwhile the teachers teach the children how to be well-adjusted to the world. The world is happy that the church is teaching the Golden Rule, because that has been its religion all along: namely, do good unto others and they'll do the same for you.

The show is obviously expensive. It is surprising how some

Christians can castigate fundamentalists, shrug off the Virgin Birth, and look askance at anyone who accepts the historic confessions literally, but when it comes to stewardship they wax almost Biblical and plainspoken. They take obvious Scriptural truths figuratively, but become gravely literalistic when it comes to extracting the tithe.

The prima donnas vie for the director's attention, and compete for his favors. Think of the average Protestant church. If the stars don't know the pastoral director, where his wife went to school, when he gets up in the morning, and how his wife keeps house, they feel they aren't "in the know," the minister isn't friendly, and they lose interest in the show.

The independent tabernacle movement has thrived as religious theater. In this type of religious vaudeville most of the activity takes place onstage, and the pastor is the producer-director of the choirs, ensembles, newly-converted ex-gangsters, and sensational visiting pulpiteers. Administrative control usually rests with the minister, some of his family and one or two dependable friends.

The advantages of the tabernacle movement are that the well-attended prayer meetings provide opportunities for discussion and small group therapy; the sensational programs are more flexible and attract a large number of unchurched souls, and persons with little education and few social skills may hear the Word without immediately being thrust into a kingdom-colony of busy beavers.

The expansive-vindictive neurotic layman never lasts long in this environment because the whole show goes smoothly onstage. There is, however, great attraction for persons with trends of detachment and pharisaism, because they can demonstrate pious merit without getting personally involved in the tabernacle program.

The person with strong trends of neurotic dependence is

attracted toward the figure of the tabernacle pastor-hero. It may be enough for him simply to be involved in the grand production, and adore the minister from afar. We have, however, interviewed a number of persons with these trends who soon turned against the pastor-hero because they were unable to make demands upon his time and condescension. On the other hand, there were some who worked industriously on the staff without pay and were rewarded with acceptance into the inner circle. One wondered who they loved more—Christ or "Our Leader"?

The theater concept drains off the church's power because it degrades the authority of the Word, limits freedom, and takes responsibility out of the hands of the many and places it into the hands of the few. It is too big a temptation to the disturbed person to play to the balcony and hope for loud and prolonged applause from fans in an appreciative audience. It makes the pastor the scapegoat for all sins, and initiates converts as spectators instead of participants.

To succeed in combating this false concept, a massive program of intensive Christian education must be initiated to dwarf anything thus far attempted. And to do it, all Christians must see that they are teachers as well as ministers and deacons. To teach, they must learn and experience the power of the Word. Christian education may be more than instruction, but it is at least that. The beckonings of our faith can only be heeded if a sound system of doctrine supports faith. We may have a lot of things to say to the world, but if we do not at least have good news from God, then we must return to grandly reciting our own plays. If we cannot re-enact the drama of crucifixion and resurrection, then we have no alternative but to intone our homemade homilies on the coming utopia.

Below are listed a few of the correctives that we feel have

some relevance to ameliorating neurosis in the church and encouraging a perspicacious program of Christian education:

1) Educate new church members in doctrine. The life in Christ demands a whole new frame of reference and wholly new resources. What does the cross mean? Why was it necessary for Christ to rise from the dead? Is the Christian immune to the world's threats which make men feel inferior and defensive? How can the anxious person undertake more responsibilities in the Kingdom when he already has enough trouble keeping his head above water? What are the meanings of the words "justified by faith and not by works"?

2) Educate new members in churchmanship. Life in the church is God's laboratory where we test the power of love and the forgiveness of God. To forgive without feeling belittled, and to love without feeling that good intentions are getting the better of common sense, are arts which must be learned in the community of mercy. We are then equipped to take into the world a heart strong enough to be wounded without going sour on life.

Building a firm foundation of Christian truth always involves the risk of isolation from the world. This is especially true for the pharisaic neurotic personality who may glue creeds and confessions all over his armor-plate defenses. He is in a quandry because he faces another one of those Christian paradoxes. On one hand, he recognizes the perils of conformity with the world and the imperative of Christian distinctiveness. On the other, he is told the church must spend herself "where cross the crowded ways of life." This tension will not be resolved in a day. The gaining of inner poise and holiness to minister without compromise will not come immediately, but classes in churchmanship will bring new members into the immediate recognition of the paradox. How One could be the glorious Messiah and still mix with harlots, drunkards and publicans, was something the Pharisees could never understand.

Put another way, confession of Christ as Saviour draws us from the world; confession of Christ as Lord sends us back into it. Too often the church has stressed salvation, with all that we receive from God. This is good for the church's comfort, peace and statistics, but she has neglected the Lordship of Christ by which we understand what God receives from us. In one case we learn the benefits of the cross; in the other we take up the cross and carry it.

The family of God contains many spoiled children who are unhappy to be told that the Christian life is not one of self-centeredness, self-righteous and self-seeking, but a life of sacrifice, service and stewardship. When we bring a soul into the church without an understanding of redemption, without a personal experience of Christ the Lord, and with little sense of urgent mission—and suddenly inform him he becomes a minister upon confirmation of baptismal vows—we make the church an epic folly in the world's eyes. The truth is, one cannot know Christ as Saviour without accepting Him as Lord of life.

The contention that we ought to impose no burdens on persons joining the church, and that they can begin to understand their public vows years after making them, has helped make the church a mission field. It is proving to be a hard field because the ground is a mass of idols. It has helped make the redemption of power blocs, vested interests, and disturbed persons a most difficult and arduous task. That is why we cannot help the neurotic religious personality without making a spiritual assault upon the weaknesses of the church which contribute to his anxiety, isolation and defensiveness. We cannot chirp a happy welcome to persons strolling into the church, as if Christ imposed no yoke whatever on His disciples. If we do, we will continue to reveal our impotence in lifting the yoke of anxiety, isolation and defensiveness off the pilgrims of the world.

When new members are trained in discipleship they carry a humility into church life which disavows any desire to remake the church into their image. They come to accept the fact that no matter how much they serve Christ, the church does not belong to them. They carry both confidence and meekness, good humor and reverence, friendliness and mutual respect into congregational ventures. They are blessings because they see the church not as a country club, but as a headquarters for a spiritual offensive. Challenged to tasks beyond them, they discover the profound peace that accompanies hard leaning on God.

3) Why is it imperative that the age for confirmation be twelve, and not fourteen or sixteen or eighteen? I have often wondered why a large body of "normal" members can only become excited about religion when they are opposed to pastor or program in a church dispute. I have concluded it is because they have grown accustomed to second-class membership, and negativism is their chief expression of a desire to be recognized. This second-class feeling goes back to confirmation. Yearning to bask in the prestige of their children's confirmation, parents made it clear that the rites should automatically take place, ready or not. The children were suddenly pronounced members after learning some religious material. But from the beginning, the church elected its officers and ironed out its complicated policies without them.

Many of these Christians, at twelve, had a deep feeling for Christ. And many of them realized they were changed by the eternal work of the Holy Spirit. Some grew, even during sixteen to nineteen, to be pillars in the church. Many more, however, were not taught the complex administration of a church; or if they were, they did not understand. In fact, by thirteen, they were not participating in congregational worship at all. At twenty or thirty, they still were not taught the place of mutual respect, forgiveness and kindness in church relationships. They carried over into the church the same sparring and bickering one finds in introverted secular societies.

At sixteen to eighteen, a young man feels free to tell his parents whether or not he is ready to shoulder the burden of the cross. Sunday school classes and youth fellowship education should teach doctrine and churchmanship, and should call for total personal commitment to Christ. If a young man is not ready, an order from his parents will not make him ready. If he happens to be ready at twelve, his continued and evident service through the Kingdom will make later confirmation an added blessing to Christ and His congregation.

Persons who make public vows and join the church are babes in the faith and not mature soldiers. Verbal confessions of faith will not suddenly make them grow up. Salvation and growth are the work of the Holy Spirit, and anyone may attend worship regularly before making such a profession. Think about the pressures on boards and pastors to place on the church rolls as many names as possible, in the shortest time, in order to inflate the statistics. And then think of the burden of guilt that hangs on the Protestant Church in the knowledge that only twenty to forty per cent of her members worship God on any one Sunday.

The Cumberland Presbyterian Church General Assembly of 1960 heard Jose D. Fajaro, director of the Collegio Americano, Cali, Colombia, declare: "The greatest temptation of the church today is to desire favor with man to such an extent that it may come to believe that when it has become the great, powerful, accepted, respected, and dominant church, it will no longer have anything to worry about."

If the church feels that she can impress culture with the power of false numbers, she will continue to be discomfited by the sight of her own running sores. The disputes and slander in the church do not grow out of a healthy response to the acceptance of the challenge of controversial issues, but out of the church's inability to solve interpersonal issues within her life which the world has not solved. She addresses herself to problems in mission which she has bypassed in Christian nurture.

Clearly, our task is to devote ourselves to prayer, study of the Scriptures and mutual edification in the fellowship of the Spirit, so that a new personal commitment may lead us to a personal rediscovery of the authority of the Word. This rediscovery will, in turn, plunge us into a teaching program that will support every buttress, every arch, every stone and every spire in the temple of God.

NOTES

Page	Line	
6	8	Harry Golden, *Enjoy, Enjoy* (Permabooks, 1960), p. 45.
16	10	Reginald Heber.
16	14	Matthew 10:34. (Scripture verses in this book are quoted from *The Revised Standard Version*, copyrighted 1946 and 1952.)
16	18	II Corinthians 10:3-4.
17	23	*The Suburban Captivity of the Churches* (Doubleday & Co., Inc., 1961), p. 100.
19	6	*Presbyterian Life* (March 1, 1961), p. 16.
19	12	*In Place of Folly* (Harper & Brothers, 1961).
25	20	C. Harry Atkinson, "What Worries Pastors Most," *Protestant Church* (February 1959), p. 11.
28	4	R. G. Riechmann, "The Christian Ministry," *Christianity Today* (May 8, 1961), p. 8.
31	16	John Lewis Gillin and John Philip Gillin, *An Introduction to Sociology* (The Macmillan Company, 1944), p. 319.
32	32	Margaret Kuhn, "Dealing With Controversy," *Social Progress* (April 1961), p. 12.
33	23	Roswell Barnes, *Under Orders* (Doubleday & Co., Inc., 1961), p. 22.
35	10	Roger L. Shinn.
37	20	Gibson Winter, *The Suburban Captivity of the Churches*, p. 67.
41	4	I Corinthians 1:26-29.
41	24	*The Acts of the Apostles* (Fleming H. Revell Company, 1924), pp. 465-466.
45	23	*What Life Should Mean to You* (Grosset & Dunlap, Inc., 1931), p. 51.
57	9	Percival M. Symonds, *The Ego and the Self* (Appleton-Century-Crofts, Inc., 1951), p. 50.
58	22	Alfred Adler, *What Life Should Mean to You*, pp. 60-61.

Page	Line	
60	19	Psalm 139:21.
63	11	Based on Karen Horney's concept of three neurotic "types." The author prefers to consider them as three poles of psychic influence, since there is no such thing as a clear-cut "type."
64	24	*Clinical Psychology* (McGraw-Hill Book Co., Inc., 1956), pp. 129-130.
65	9	Karen Horney, *Neurosis and Human Growth* (W. W. Norton & Co., Inc., 1950), p. 97.
65	24	*Ibid.*, p. 195.
70	18	*Ibid.*, p. 201.
77	33	I Peter 5:5 (*King James Version*).
79	19	Karen Horney, *Our Inner Conflicts* (W. W. Norton & Co., Inc., 1945), p. 292.
85	1	*Christ and Selfhood* (Association Press, 1961), p. 67.
92	18	Dolores Barracano Schmidt, *Ladies' Home Journal,* n.d.
95	26	*Neurosis and Human Growth,* p. 246.
99	19	*Christ and Selfhood,* p. 48.
102	17	Elliott Dunlap Smith, "Conflict Between Duties and Major Values," *Pastoral Psychology* (October 1961), p. 19.
103	8	Graham R. Hodges, "Shattering the Composite Pastor Image," *Pulpit Digest* (September 1961), p. 42.
104	15	"The Pastor's Personal Witness to the Faith," *Pastoral Psychology* (November 1960), pp. 29-32.
105	10	Raymond T. Stramm, *The Interpreter's Bible* (Abingdon Press, 1953), Vol. X, p. 558.
105	16	*Ibid.*
105	30	*Ibid.,* p. 566.
114	3	Fritz Kunkel, *Conquer Yourself* (Ives Washburn, Inc., 1936), pp. 278-279.
118	13	*Our Inner Conflicts,* p. 76.
121	3	Romans 7:24.
121	8	Romans 4:24.
127	26	*Word and Sacrament* (Prentice-Hall, Inc., 1961).
130	25	*A Dictionary of the Bible* (The John C. Winston Company, 1948), p. 508.
132	19	Galatians 5:14-15.

Page	Line	
136	17	John 3:8.
146	12	*The Status Seekers* (David McKay Co., Inc., 1959).
147	10	II Corinthians 3:17-18.
150	21	Acts 7:51-52.
160	2	"Our Demanding Laity," *Christianity Today* (September 15, 1958), pp. 14-15.
170	29	Matthew 5:9.
179	15	Luke 6:26.
189	17	*Protestantism* (Doubleday & Co., Inc., 1928), p. 1.
193	14	John 7:47.
197	23	Hebrews 2:8-9.
198	13	*The Princeton Seminary Bulletin* (November 1960).
201	13	Isaiah 9:14-16.
203	1	Romans 10:14.
203	11	Frederick Keller Stamm, *The Best of Charles E. Jefferson* (Thomas Y. Crowell Co., 1960), p. 181.
217	24	*Pastoral Problems* (Fleming H. Revell Company, 1959), pp. 114-115.
217	28	*Ibid.,* pp. 115-116.
218	33	*Institutes,* trans. by John Allen, 7th American edition (Presbyterian Board of Christian Education, n.d.), Vol. II, p. 506.
229	16	From a paper presented at the National Council of Churches Conference on "The Ministry and the Laity," March 29, 1961.
230	5	II Corinthians 4:7.
237	24	Matthew 28:19-20.
241	28	From the hymn by Frank Mason North.